CRITICAL SOCIAL THEORY

GUIDES TO
THEOLOGICAL
INQUIRY

Edited by Kathryn Tanner of the University of Chicago and Paul Lakeland of Fairfield University, Guides to Theological Inquiry are intended to introduce students, scholars, clergy, and theologians to those academic methods, disciplines, and movements that are most germane to contemporary theology. Neither simple surveys nor exhaustive monographs, these short books provide solid, reliable, programmatic statements of the main lines or workings of their topics and assessments of their theological importance.

Already available are *Nonfoundationalism* by John E. Thiel, *Literary Theory* by David Dawson, *Postmodernity* by Paul Lakeland, *Theories of Culture* by Kathryn Tanner, and *Feminist Theory and Christian Theology* by Serene Jones. Forthcoming titles in the series include *Hermeneutics* by Francis Schüssler Fiorenza, *African American Critical Thought* by Shawn Copeland, and *Historicism in Theology* by Sheila Greeve Davaney.

CRITICAL SOCIAL THEORY

PROPHETIC REASON, CIVIL SOCIETY, AND CHRISTIAN IMAGINATION

GARY M. SIMPSON

GUIDES TO THEOLOGICAL INQUIRY

FORTRESS PRESS / MINNEAPOLIS

For
Edward H. Schroeder and Robert W. Bertram
professors, prophets, parishioners

CRITICAL SOCIAL THEORY
Prophetic Reason, Civil Society, and Christian Imagination
Guides to Theological Inquiries series

Scripture quotations are from the New Revised Standard Version Bible, copyright © 1989 by the Division of Christian Education of the National Council of the Churches of Christ in the USA and used by permission.

Cover design: Craig Claeys
Text design: David Lott
Cover photo: © 1997 Tony Stone Images

Library of Congress Cataloging-in-Publication Data
Simpson, Gary M.
    Critical social theory : prophetic reason, civil society, and Christian imagination / Gary M. Simpson
        p. cm. — (Guides to theological inquiry)
    Includes bibliographical references and index.
    ISBN 0–8006–2916–7 (alk. paper)
    1. Sociology, Christian. I. Title. II. Series.

BT738.S553 2001
261.8'01—dc21   2001040451

The paper used in this publication meets the minimum requirements of American National Standard for Information Sciences — Permanence of Paper for Printed Library Materials, ANSI Z329.48-1984.

Manufactured in the U.S.A.   AF 1–2916

05   04   03   02   1   2   3   4   5   6   7   8   9   10

Contents

Part Three. Prophetic Reason and Communicative Imagination

Foreword

Whether it is mere failure of nerve or a genuine and seismic shift in the intellectual landscape, today we have trouble finding our way around in the world of ideas. In the past, it was always *terra firma*. True, there might have been potholes, swamps, and even dragons, but there were maps to designate the precise locations in which these and other dangers to the traveler might be found. In our age, there can be no maps, because there is no agreement on what the terrain looks like, or even if there is any terrain at all. From the Copernican revolution that substituted the sun for the earth as the center of the Universe, through the discoveries of modern physics and astronomy, we know now—cosmologically, philosophically, and culturally—that there is no center.

It is this pervasive sense of the absence of center, security, or certainty, and its profound implications for theology and the study of religion, that the Guides to Theological Inquiry exist to investigate. Each volume in the series takes up one important theme in contemporary theological investigation and religious studies. No mere surveys, these texts aim to make constructive proposals for the theological usefulness of their particular focus.

Gary Simpson initiates a dialogue between critical social theory and the Protestant prophetic imagination. On the one hand, he charts the emergence of an understanding of critical theory in the work of the Frankfurt School, principally in the thought of Max Horkheimer, and shows how Jürgen Habermas's views both correct and advance the notion of critical theory into a full-fledged philosophical and political account of the contemporary world. On the other, and interwoven with this, is the fascinating story of Paul Tillich's early associations with the Frankfurt School, and the dialectical relationship between the notion of critical theory and Tillich's views on prophetic criticism. This emerges in an important constructive proposal for the role of contemporary Christian congregations as "public companions," which restores the prophetical dimension to the notion of servanthood. Simpson's work is important for the continued understanding of Christian relevance to the postmodern world. It offers a stimulating reading of critical theory, will give new vigor to debates on the social role of Christianity, and above all shows the fruitfulness of continued dialogue between secular and religious thought.

—Paul Lakeland

Preface

Come now, let us argue it out,
says the Lord . . .

Isaiah 1:18

In the summer of 1969 I rocked for hours in the same chair on the same porch that Great Grandpa Winterstein had rocked in for over eight decades. I had just finished my freshman year in college and one of my spring quarter courses had been a class in "Social Problems," complete with immersion events in Detroit's "black" culture. I aspired, awkwardly, to continue the immersion. First on my summer reading list were Martin Luther King, Jr.'s "Letter from Birmingham Jail" and the other essays in *Why We Can't Wait,* and Malcolm X's *The Autobiography of Malcolm X.*[1] I took to that rocking chair every hour when not working my summer job. I was incapable of putting Martin and Malcolm down! King christened summer 1963 "the summer of our discontent"[2] and by summer 1967 the streets of Detroit were aflame with rage. Summer 1969 would be a summer of *my* discontent. And so would the next.

During June 1970 I went on a marvelous college choir tour of western Europe. We visited many of its grand old cities. Along with cathedrals and museums and pubs of various kinds we journeyed to the Nazi concentration camp at Dachau, Germany. It was surely a long journey from my front porch—still is. A few days after visiting Dachau, I spent the night in a farmer's house in Gols, Austria, a mere half a mile from the barbed wire of the iron curtain with its guard tower keeping watch over us by night. In the morning we all got together and sang "America the Beautiful" and the "Star Spangled Banner" while the guards peered at us through their binoculars. I sang heartily, and still do, though modulated by discontent, sometimes rage.

Rage—one would not be too far adrift to describe the twentieth century as the age of the rage of nations. Since 1989 rage erupts as often within national borders as it does between nations. Today the rage of nations percolates internally in the United States as well as many places throughout the globe—even in the heartland of the Midwest where I am now located. It percolates through the very capillaries of everyday life. The metaphors that saturate our daily discourse sign it: "culture wars," "the disuniting of America," "the melting pot at boiling point," "drive-by politics," "hate radio," "school violence," "virtual kiddie porn." Will we celebrate the "fall of the wall" of 1989 and so soon ignore the age of capillary rage and its globalization? Something deeply moral and manifold is at stake in this capillary rage. As a moral, indeed, as a prophetic thermometer, it measures the decreasing possibility for the good life of an increasing number of ordinary residents. Indeed a good society is at stake:

> cease to do evil,
>   learn to do good;
> seek justice,
>   rescue the oppressed,
> defend the orphan,
>   plead for the widow.
> Isaiah 1:16-17

In "Letter from Birmingham Jail" King agitated the churches' transformation from public opinion thermometer to prophetic thermostat. Being relocated to prophetic imagination is as encumbering as the journey from Great Grandpa Winterstein's rocker to Birmingham and Dachau and Gols. How true this is for Christian congregations King surely knew.[3] Why is it, though, that so many clergy and other leaders posit, unlike King, that they must practice the prophetic imagination in direct proportion to their distance from local congregations?[4] Robert Michael Franklin for one resists that assumption and I take his resistance as my cue for this book.[5] *How might Christians practice the prophetic imagination in direct proportion to their closeness to local congregations?* This aspiration forms the subtext of my exploration of critical social theory. *Indeed, critical social theory, oriented around its communicative turn, can assist Christian theology to retrieve the prophetic imagination for a newly emerging missional era of Christian congregations in North America.* If, as has been said, critical social theory was a creation of the early 1930s and a discovery of the late 1960s, how then might its development in the 1980s and 1990s aid our retrieval of the prophetic imagination for the challenges of the twenty-first century?[6]

Our exploration is divided into three major parts. Part one, in two chapters, probes the "genesis" of critical social theory, also called the Frankfurt School, and the initial Christian theological "engagement" with it. Part two, in three chapters, depicts the "critical" transformation of the Frankfurt School oriented around a thoroughly communicative "theory" for a decolonizing, emancipatory "society" rooted in a civil society that makes a deliberative democracy and a stakeholder economy possible. In a concluding chapter, part three retrieves certain features of the initial Christian engagement—prophetic reason and concrete congregations—and develops these through critical social theory's communicative turn for a new era of missional congregations that includes a prophetic vocation of public companionship.

> though your sins are like scarlet,
>   they shall be like snow;
> though they are red like crimson,
>   they shall become like wool.
> If you are willing and obedient,
>   you shall eat the good of the land;
> but if you refuse and rebel,
>   you shall be devoured by the sword;
>   for the mouth of the Lord has spoken.
>   Isaiah 1:18-20

I want to thank several colleagues who have read parts of this book and offered suggestions: David Fredrickson, Lee Snook, and Patrick Keifert. I also appreciate the assistance that I have received from Alice Loddigs, Steve Turnbull, and Donavon Riley. Finally, my heartfelt thanks go to my wife, Sharon Geiger, and our three daughters, Lara, Elena, and Krista, who in untold ways brought encouragement along the way.

Abbreviations

AS   Jürgen Habermas, *Autonomy and Solidarity: Interviews with Jürgen Habermas,* ed. P. Dews, rev. ed. (London: Verso, 1992).

BFN   Jürgen Habermas, *Between Facts and Norms: Contributions to a Discourse Theory of Law and Democracy,* trans. W. Rehg (Cambridge, Mass.: MIT Press, 1996).

BPSS   Max Horkheimer, *Between Philosophy and Social Science: Selected Early Writings,* trans. G. Hunter, M. Kramer, and J. Torpey (Cambridge, Mass.: MIT Press, 1995).

CES   Jürgen Habermas, *Communication and the Evolution of Society,* trans. T. McCarthy (Boston: Beacon Press, 1979).

CT   Max Horkheimer, *Critical Theory: Selected Essays,* trans. M. O'Connell et al. (New York: Seabury Press, 1972).

DD   Max Horkheimer, *Dawn and Decline: Notes, 1926–1931 and 1950–1969,* trans. M. Shaw (New York: Seabury Press, 1978).

DE   Max Horkheimer and Theodor Adorno, *Dialectic of Enlightenment,* trans. J. Cumming (New York: Continuum, 1995).

EME   Jürgen Habermas, "The Entwinement of Myth and Enlightenment: Re-reading *Dialectic of Enlightenment,*" trans. T. Levin, *New German Critique* 26 (spring/summer 1982): 11–30.

ER   Max Horkheimer, *Eclipse of Reason* (New York: Seabury Press, 1974).

FRPS   Jürgen Habermas, "Further Reflections on the Public Sphere," in *Habermas and the Public Sphere,* ed. C. Calhoun (Cambridge, Mass.: MIT Press, 1992), 421–61.

JA   Jürgen Habermas, *Justification and Application: Remarks on Discourse Ethics,* trans. C. Cronin (Cambridge, Mass.: MIT Press, 1993).

KHI   Jürgen Habermas, *Knowledge and Human Interests,* trans. J. Shapiro (Boston: Beacon Press, 1971).

MCCA Jürgen Habermas, *Moral Consciousness and Communicative Action,* trans. C. Lenhardt and S. Weber Nicholsen (Cambridge, Mass.: MIT Press, 1990).

ABBREVIATIONS xiii

NC	Jürgen Habermas, *The New Conservatism: Cultural Criticism and the Historians' Debate*, trans. S. Weber Nicholsen (Cambridge, Mass.: MIT Press, 1989).
OHCU	Jürgen Habermas, "On Hermeneutics' Claim to Universality," in *The Hermeneutic Reader: Texts of the German Tradition from the Enlightenment to the Present*, ed. K. Mueller-Vollmer (New York: Continuum, 1997), 294–319.
OLSS	Jürgen Habermas, *On the Logic of the Social Sciences*, trans. S. Weber Nicholsen and J. Stark (Cambridge, Mass.: MIT Press, 1991).
PCCP	Paul Tillich, "Protestantism as a Critical and Creative Principle," in *Political Expectation* (New York: Harper & Row, 1971).
PDM	Jürgen Habermas, *The Philosophical Discourse of Modernity: Twelve Lectures*, trans. F. Lawrence (Cambridge, Mass.: MIT Press, 1987).
PE	Paul Tillich, *The Protestant Era*, trans. J. L. Adams (Chicago: University of Chicago Press, 1957).
PPP	Jürgen Habermas, *Philosophical-Political Profiles*, trans. F. Lawrence (Cambridge, Mass.: MIT Press, 1985).
PT	Jürgen Habermas, *Postmetaphysical Thinking: Philosophical Essays*, trans. W. Hohengarten (Cambridge, Mass.: MIT Press, 1992).
RRR	Paul Tillich, review of *Reason and Revolution: Hegel and the Rise of Revolution*, by Herbert Marcuse, *Studies in Philosophy and Social Science* 9 (1941): 476–78.
STPS	Jürgen Habermas, *The Structural Transformation of the Public Sphere: An Inquiry into a Category of Bourgeois Society*, trans. T. Burger and F. Lawrence (Cambridge, Mass.: MIT Press, 1989).
TCA 1	Jürgen Habermas, *The Theory of Communicative Action*, vol. 1: *Reason and the Rationalization of Society*, trans. T. McCarthy (Boston: Beacon Press, 1984).
TCA 2	Jürgen Habermas, *The Theory of Communicative Action*, vol. 2: *Lifeworld and System*, trans. T. McCarthy (Boston: Beacon Press, 1988).
TCT	Max Horkheimer, "Traditional and Critical Theory," in *Critical Theory: Selected Essays*, trans. M. O'Connell et al. (New York: Seabury Press, 1972), 188–243.
TP	Jürgen Habermas, *Theory and Practice*, trans. J. Viertel (Boston: Beacon Press, 1973).

PART ONE

Critical Social Theory
and Christian Imagination—
Genesis and Engagement

1

Horkheimer:
The Idea of Critical Social Theory

From its beginning, critical social theory showed a restlessness toward the reigning division of labor within the academic disciplines at German universities. This division of labor both mirrored and contributed, mightily, to German culture, society, and politics, and, thus, to the everyday life of ordinary German people. With a desire to overcome this reigning division of labor, the critical theorists developed their theory of society as a hybrid of sorts. We sort out the hybrid nature of their project by examining critical social theory step by step.

The genesis of critical theory's hybrid nature goes back to Max Horkheimer's appointment in 1930 as director of the Institute of Social Research at the University of Frankfurt. Along with the directorship of the institute came a university teaching position. Since the institute specialized in social research, the expected appointment was to be in sociology. Horkheimer, however, was a philosopher by training. Still, an appointment to a philosophy chair would not do since he focused on both the *social* sources and the *social* consequences of philosophy. Horkheimer argued that the illusory abstraction of philosophical reflection from its social context was a practiced delusion, sometimes intentional and sometimes not. The university's philosophy department at the time practiced a more conventional discipline of philosophy that did not accommodate Horkheimer's focus. Creation of a new kind of chair was needed, a hybrid of sociology and philosophy. The university established a chair in *social* philosophy and gave the appointment to Horkheimer.[1]

The hybrid nature of critical social theory goes beyond a blending of philosophy and sociology. As we shall see, Horkheimer considered both philosophy and sociology, as then practiced, ill equipped to help Germany escape its drive toward Nazi fascism. He eventually came to consider both the philosophers and their philosophy, and the sociologists and their sociology, to be, at best, compliant with and, at worst, conspiratorial with Nazism. In Germany during the first quarter of the twentieth century, two prominent schools of philosophy did highlight social reality: Edmund Husserl's phenomenology and Max Scheler's *Lebensphilosophie* (philosophy of life). Both of these socially sensitive philosophical orientations, however, disdained sociological research for what, in the 1920s, was a rigid empiricist bent. Horkheimer, too, rejects the empiricist commitments of that kind of sociological research. Nevertheless, and in contrast to Husserl and Scheler, he perceives the potential value of encompassing research into social realities.

The institute's model of social research, as Horkheimer began his appointment, would have to be free from the empiricism that had dominated the study of society up until that time. As our story will reveal, only by means of emancipation from empiricism could social philosophy highlight the "constant connection to real life" that inspired Horkheimer. In fact, he always insisted on interpreting every philosophy also as a "social" philosophy. Every philosopher, he argued, has an interest in and ideas about the social world, no matter how abstracting, otherworldly, or obfuscating—or how simple and commonsensical—the philosophy appears. This insistence on the real-life contexts *and* consequences of every philosophy marks Horkheimer's thinking at every turn and remains a hallmark of critical theory.[2] As we shall see, Horkheimer thinks that social philosophy will also have to be freed from atomistic individualism.

Horkheimer's focus on "real life" comes as no afterthought for him and the other members of the Frankfurt institute's research team. They were all Jews in a Germany rapidly coming under Hitler's influence. No wonder that their critical theory's ultimate aim is the philosophical interpretation of the vicissitudes of human fate—the fate of humans not merely as individuals, but as members of a community. Above all, therefore, critical theory attends to phenomena that can only be understood in the context of human social life, to the state, law, economy, and religion—in short, to the entire material and intellectual culture of humanity.[3]

Because the institute engaged in sociological research, we begin our story at the birthplace of modern sociology and in the social world that it identified. Second, we listen in on Horkheimer's conversations and arguments with the "traditional" theory that emerged with modern sociology. Finally, we accompany Horkheimer as he learns from and disagrees with three predecessors. In this way we discover how Horkheimer's critical theory of society developed through the 1930s. I reserve the development of his ideas after 1940 for chapter 3.

The Genesis of Sociology

Modern sociology began in the first quarter of the nineteenth century with two French thinkers, Henri Saint-Simon and Auguste Comte.[4] As they reflected on the problems facing French society during the restoration following the French Revolution and the defeat of Napoleon, they immediately drew their attention to an emerging class of people. Saint-Simon called them the *productive industriel*. The old feudal society had consisted of two classes, commoners and aristocracy. As feudalism wore on, certain groups of artisans, industrialists, and scientists—Saint-Simon's *productive industriel*—emerged from within the class of commoners.

These groups outclassed, so to speak, the commoners from whose loins they had come. Still, these new groups could not just "become" members of the aristocracy. You became an aristocrat the old-fashioned way, by having been "born" an aristocrat. These emerging groups were not aristocrats, though some would pretend to be. But they were not exactly commoners, whom they would soon begin to loathe. Rather, these emerging groups were forming, unknown to anyone, a class of their own, a "middle" class. How shall this nondescript "middle"—those who were not commoners or aristocrats—be described? One factor stood out plainly; this "middle" had taken up the cause of the Revolution. By analyzing this new phenomenon in Western society, Saint-Simon and Comte set off on a journey to a new science—the science of society, or sociology, as Comte would call it.

Prior to the Revolution, the aristocracy merely tolerated this emerging middle class. Soon, however, the aristocracy realized the "usefulness" of individual members of the middle class for perpetuating the aristocratic way of life. Members of the middle class quickly internalized this value of individual usefulness as a basis for their difference from commoners. Eventually, they would see their individual utility as a reason to dislodge the aristocracy itself from its social preeminence, and they followed through by supporting the Revolution. After the Revolution decimated the aristocracy, the middle class obviously could no longer define itself through its usefulness to the upper class. Saint-Simon saw the dilemma and seized the opportunity. He sought to convince both the middle class and the aristocracy to transform middle-class allegiance to utility into something different.

From the beginning, Saint-Simon displayed ambivalence toward this middle-class utilitarian culture. On the one hand, his thinking rested on a powerful distinction between the useful and the useless. If the middle class were to remain useful, their utility, since the aristocracy had been weakened by the Revolution, would have to be transferred from the aristocracy to some other entity. The middle class would have to be useful for the French nation as a whole and even for humanity itself. On the other hand, Saint-Simon remained critical of the middle class's "individualistic" utilitarianism, which, to be sure, the aristocracy was able to exploit for its own benefits.

The transference of middle-class usefulness to the nation and humanity necessitated a new conceptualization of middle-class utility. Saint-Simon marked two factors as crucial for the transformation. First, the middle class would have to become aware of its "social" utility, that is, its usefulness as a class for the coherence and solidarity of the social whole. This idea represents the extent of Saint-Simon's own "socialism." While some of his followers leaned toward a "utopian" socialism, he did not, and neither would Comte. Rather, Saint-Simon labored to locate *what* among the middle class could inflate in social value to be useful to the whole.

Saint-Simon postulated that the middle class's knowledge—more precisely, its *way of knowing*—would ascend in value. Once the middle class focused on its utilitarian consequences for the social whole, thought Saint-Simon, it would discover the importance of its knowledge for its genesis and success as a class. Ironically, middle-class usefulness resides in its unique way of knowing what is consequential, in knowing what is useful. As a hunch, Saint-Simon contemplated a model of knowing social consequences that was patterned after the natural sciences, which had made impressive strides over the previous 150 years in acquiring knowledge of the natural world.

The twofold dedication to social utility and to science suggested a science of society based on the empirical knowledge of factual consequences. Conceptualizing such a science of society fell to one of Saint-Simon's star pupils, Auguste Comte. Comte's sociology followed the general trajectory of *scientific positivism,* the term used by Saint-Simon. Comte developed sociological positivism within the context of the restoration. During this period, following the defeat of Napoleon, the aristocratic elite sought to restore its control of France. But no fundamental social consensus existed. A severe struggle for society-wide hegemony ensued between the aristocracy and the middle class. Each class suffered serious internal fragmentation; furthermore, the previous decades of unrest had hurt the credibility of the French Catholic Church. During the restoration, the church again lent its support to the aristocracy, and this partisanship eliminated Catholicism as a source for a new social consensus. The search for a new social glue began.

Comte noticed that the natural sciences alone were gaining broad-based public respect and support. Further, he recognized that the tenets of the natural sciences did not derive from the convictions of social class or from the church. In a stroke of genius, though a fateful one from the perspective of critical social theory, Comte, following the hunch of Saint-Simon, turned to the natural sciences as a model for fashioning a new French consensus regarding society. By adopting the apolitical and yet "positive" convictions attached to the natural sciences, Comte dreamed of restoring social order.

Comte's positivism consisted of six dominant characteristics. First, *positivism,* unlike the Enlightenment, is "positive" rather than negative. From Comte's perspective, Enlightenment thinking continuously and too resolutely bends itself toward critique, toward debunking other ways of thinking. Second, positivism would not project such a negative character because, as Comte asserted, it rests on "positively" certain knowledge gained through rigorous scientific method rather than on dubious knowledge gained either through religious revelation or philosophical speculation. As we will see, Horkheimer scrutinizes both of these "positive" characteristics of positivism on the way toward formulating a critical theory of society. Three other elements coalesced at the center of Comte's positivism. Positivism concentrates on the social rather than the individual, it remains apolitically detached rather than politically partisan, and it tends toward maintaining order rather than propelling change. Horkheimer also focuses on these enduring aspects of positivism.

Comte presented positivism as a new map of social order, as a "religion of humanity," as he called it. This represents the sixth basic feature of positivism. The religiosity of this feature would come and go with positivism's various reincarnations, but even when this feature manifested itself, it usually remained subsidiary. Comte himself would later surrender the religiosity of positivism.

What survived, indeed, what thrived, through all permutations of positivism was the focus on social order. Struggles clearly existed between the aristocracy and the middle class during the French restoration. Still, since the Revolution, the momentum of social ascendancy remained with the middle class. Comte's twofold slogan, "Order and Progress," won their hearts. They desired the present order because they were dominant, and they desired progress as the way to maintain, increase, and insure their dominance. They presumed, thereby, that the present social order would remain sound even if incomplete. As Comte's positivism progressively became coupled with the middle class, it came more and more to serve the interests of the middle class. From its conception, positivism left limited room for criticizing the inadequacies of the social whole. This increasing fixation on the soundness of the reigning social order joined with the ahistorical doctrine of "the fact," isolating the present condition from the past or the future. As we shall see, Horkheimer's enthusiastic quest for a new theory of society, for a *critical theory,* arises because the devotion to maintain the reigning Nazi social order converges with the natural-science doctrine of "facts."

Traditional "Positivist" Theory

Not until the 1937 essay "Traditional and Critical Theory" did Horkheimer coin the term *critical theory* and use it for the overall project of the Institute of Social Research.[5] To be sure, he had conceptualized much of a critical theory of society in the six or seven years prior to 1937. Before 1937, he usually referred to the institute's work as "materialism." Over the years he became increasingly aware of the inadequacy of "materialism" to identify the institute's overall project. The reasons will become clear below.

The closing paragraph of this now-famous essay draws attention to the convergence between Germany's fascism and positivism.

> In a historical period like the present true theory is more critical than affirmative. . . . Mankind has already been abandoned by a science which in its imaginary self-sufficiency thinks of the shaping of [social and political] practice, which it [unthinkingly] serves and to which it [unconsciously] belongs, simply as something lying outside its borders and is content with this separation of thought and action.[6]

This convergence did not arise by accident. Horkheimer suspects that the "traditional" theory of positivism not only allowed fascism to thrive but also that positivism's most basic tenets served to maintain and, indeed, to promote fascism.[7] Traditional positivism's "achievements are incorporated into the apparatus of society; [its] achievements are a factor in the conservation and continuous renewal of the existing state of affairs."[8]

Horkheimer fashions a "true" theory of society, a critical theory, by positioning himself in the midst of a four-hundred-year-old conversation and argument between "traditional theory" and predecessors of his critical theory. In "traditional theory," Horkheimer includes empiricism and what he calls the bourgeois philosophy of history. In the theories of critique he includes Immanuel Kant, Georg Hegel, and Karl Marx. Each theory of critique, however, retained elements of traditional theory and, thereby, argues Horkheimer, remained flawed. Above all, Horkheimer hones in on the *social* world that both traditional theory and the theories of critique promoted even—and especially—when they did not acknowledge that they were promoting a particular social arrangement.

Agreements with Traditional Theory

Horkheimer perceives a difference between early traditional positivism and its later positivistic heirs. He classifies the emerging seventeenth- and eighteenth-century natural sciences as early positivism.[9] He maintains a substantial agreement with "early positivism," because its knowledge claims contrasted with those that predominated in medieval feudalism. This contrast proved liberative in two "real-life" ways.

First, nature exacted a toll on the masses of people in feudal society. They suffered tremendous natural miseries due primarily to epidemics, infections, and natural disasters like famines, floods, and earthquakes. Christian metaphysics and theology, the reigning medieval forms of knowledge, seemed helpless to intervene in the calamities caused by nature. The dominant forms of medieval Christian metaphysics and theology had adopted Aristotelian philosophy. Aristotle investigated how things in the world moved, and he enumerated four possible "causes" for such movement: *formal* causes, *material* causes, *efficient* causes, and *final* causes. While Christian metaphysics and theology acknowledged all four modes, it focused on *final causation*. Movement in the world happens preeminently because of an entity's final destination, goal, or end. Medieval Christian metaphysics and theology identified God as this definitive causative factor. Even at the start of the twenty-first century, we still "acknowledge" natural calamities—and, at times, natural benefits—as "acts of God." *Formal causation* received some attention in selected versions of medieval Christian "knowledge" in that the form of God, the image or wisdom or *logos* of God, informs the shape of certain entities in the world. Nevertheless, by focusing primarily on *final causation,* Christian metaphysics and theology deemphasized the other modes of causation, particularly *material* and *efficient* causations.

In contrast to medieval Christian knowledge, the emerging natural sciences focused their attention both on the "material" that comprises the natural world (Aristotle's *material causation*) and on Aristotle's *efficient causation*. In modern usage, people have generally come to think about "cause" solely in light of Aristotle's *efficient causation*—the bumping of one billiard ball against another, resulting in the motion of the latter. Investigating *material* and *efficient* causation becomes valuable when we observe causes that recur regularly. When we see regular patterns of causation, we discover a lawfulness in nature. This premise of an orderliness to nature's workings represents a "belief in uniformity," which I discuss below.[10]

Those in the sixteenth and seventeenth centuries who investigated this kind of knowledge initiated the scientific revolution, a knowledge revolution of no small proportions.[11] Inquiry into these kinds of causes—soon to be known simply as "natural causes"—stimulated interest in developing tools that could intervene in the natural chain of events and that could alter the otherwise regularly recurring chain and its predictable, lawlike outcomes. The burgeoning natural sciences could, given enough knowledge of the material and efficient factors and the right tools for intervention, avoid natural calamities or at least soften their blow. Early positivism increasingly provided a measure of control over naturally occurring miseries and, thereby, liberated the "real life" of feudal peoples. Horkheimer finds this scenario reasonable and liberative. Eventually, however, this liberative scenario, as Horkheimer sees it, was inverted. The natural sciences and technology would come to dominate nature in order to preempt natural human miseries.

Critical theory agrees with early positivism for a second "real-life" reason. Nature is not the only factor behind human misery. Social factors contribute to misery, or at least to its distribution. Because medieval metaphysics and theology had claimed total authority and competence, they retained command of social knowledge as well. Metaphysics and theology knew the true design of society. The reigning social knowledge legitimized feudalism, consisting of a rigidly divided class structure based on birth. This knowledge made the huddled masses highly susceptible to natural calamities and lessened the misery of the aristocracy. The natural sciences, by increasingly intervening in nature and thereby relaxing Christendom's grip on natural knowledge, likewise interrupted Christendom's command of social knowledge. Early positivism noticed that medieval Christendom's social knowledge created unequal protection from natural calamities and thus contributed to the misery among the lower classes. The earliest pre-positivists of the fifteenth century had already aligned themselves with the emerging social structure based no longer on one's birth but on the usefulness of one's skill, labor, and effort. As noted earlier, the nineteenth-century fathers of positivist sociology would do the same. Horkheimer applauds the "original fruitfulness" of this emerging bourgeois way of life.[12]

Disagreements with Traditional Theory

While finding reasons to agree with early positivism, Horkheimer, nevertheless, finds "real-life" reasons to disagree with it. In his investigations of early positivism, he discovers that a latent and repressive underside adhered to its liberative aspects. As time goes on, this underside asserted itself more aggressively and eventually came to dominate. Horkheimer exposes the two layers of traditional theory that together comprised the underside: one was *empiricism,* the other was the bourgeois philosophy of history.[13]

Empiricism and its roots in rationalism. Empiricism was a theory about *what* is knowable as well as *how* these "whats" are known. The journey toward empiricism began with René Descartes in the early and mid–seventeenth century. This beginning might seem odd because Descartes was a rationalist, and empiricists offered empiricism as the alternative to *rationalism.* While this assumption about empiricists is true in some ways, it is not, as Horkheimer argues, true in others.

Descartes's rationalist ideas began as he pondered the great natural-science discoveries of the latter sixteenth and early seventeenth centuries. He himself was a natural scientist who studied how eyes worked and what caused them not to work. As Descartes meditated about his own research, he concluded that he could only know with certainty two kinds of things, because only two kinds of things were real: extending things and thinking things, bodies and minds.[14] Furthermore, minds and bodily matter are so radically different that they stand independent of each other. According to Descartes, therefore, the mind produces true knowledge out of its innate capabilities and resources. Mind's "pure" thought—"pure" reason—exists purified of bodily material, untainted by experiences that the body's senses may receive from other bodily or natural material. In this way the mind is innately pure and productive. In contrast to the mind's innate, pure, and productive knowledge, the body's sensory experiences of other bodily material seem murky and mutable, and, therefore, as Descartes saw things, not sources of "knowledge."

Ironically, Descartes's mind-and-body "dualism" prevailed as the fundamental premise of empiricism. The empiricists, like David Hume and John Locke, were skeptical that the mind consisted of the innate, productive capabilities ascribed to it by Descartes. They inverted Descartes's dualism; they did not, however, abolish it. They depicted the mind as a passive entity, a "blank slate," which simply registers with complete accuracy the senses' experiences of the external world's material data.[15] By minimizing the productive power of mind, the empiricists inflated the data of the senses to "facts," "pure facts," and "just the facts." Empiricists thought that "facts," untainted by mental meddling, exist. Horkheimer refers to this empiricist fixation as the "hypostatization" of facts.[16]

According to empiricism, mind exists in all persons, but commonly as a sloppy bundle of sense experiences. Empirical science brings "objectivity" to this bundle of sense experiences and, thus, provides "knowledge." It brings objectivity by starting with the bundle of sense data recorded in the mind and, in a disciplined manner, progressively eliminates the substantive differences among the data until it arrives at its universal features. In other words, empiricism moves inductively from the particular to the general through abstraction.[17]

Empiricists of the late seventeenth century and throughout the eighteenth century theorized that their scenario about knowledge—its *what* and *how*—represented the working model of the natural scientists of the sixteenth and early seventeenth centuries. The next generation, the nineteenth-century empiricists, further inflated the earlier "theory" about knowledge. These latter-day empiricists, true to the empiricist focus on "facts," simply assumed that the empiricist scenario of knowledge was itself an empirical fact.[18]

As if this inflationary trend were not bad enough, Horkheimer noticed another important characteristic of empiricism. The orderliness of nature, which the natural scientists observed, led empiricists not only to believe in the uniformity of nature but also to depict nature as a machine. This "mechanistic doctrine of nature" proved debilitating not only to the natural sciences but also, and especially, to the nascent sciences of society. The social sciences, as noted, used as their model the empiricist scenario of the natural sciences.[19] While Locke and Hume, true to their liberal leanings in the bourgeois era, left room for a knowing subject, twentieth-century "empiricism rejects the notion of the subject *in toto*."[20]

Horkheimer realizes how the mechanistic doctrine, combined with the empiricist eradication of the subject, desecrates real social life.

> [The] limiting of scientific activity to the description, classification, and generalization of phenomena [left science] with no care to distinguish the unimportant from the essential. . . . Scientific method was oriented to being and not becoming, and the form of society at the time was regarded as a mechanism which ran in an unvarying fashion. The mechanism might be disturbed for a shorter or longer period, but in any event it did not require a different scientific approach than did the explanation of any complicated piece of machinery.[21]

This combination toughens a world whose magnificent exterior radiates unity and order while panic and distress prevail beneath.

Autocrats, cruel colonial governors, and sadistic prison wardens have always wished for subjects with this positivistic neutrality. If science follows empiricism's lead and the intellect renounces its probing, science will be participating passively in injustice.[22]

Horkheimer fears that the commonsense perception of ordinary people in bourgeois society merely corresponded to and, indeed, reflected dominant empiricist epistemology. Ordinary people perceived their given world "as a sum-total of facts; it is there and must be accepted." Critical theory, Horkheimer writes, must develop a new epistemology as well as a new "critical" understanding of the "knowing individual as such."[23] Still, "critical theory . . . never aims simply at an increase of knowledge as such. Its goal is man's [sic] emancipation from enslaving conditions."[24] Horkheimer embarks on his critical epistemology by considering the critical philosophy of Kant. Before considering Horkheimer's encounter with Kant, we enrich the story line with a related issue.

The bourgeois philosophy of history. Horkheimer defines the bourgeois philosophy of history as elucidation of "the determinate needs, desires, exigencies, and contradictions of that [bourgeois] society."[25] He begins with Niccolò Machiavelli's *psychological* conception of history and proceeds to Thomas Hobbes's new *doctrine of natural law,* which builds on Machiavelli's understanding. The mark of their originality lay in taking key insights from the development of the sciences of nature and conceptualizing the history of society and politics through these insights.

As scientific analysis made possible the human control and domination of nature, rather than the reverse, so Machiavelli's new science of politics aspired to analyze the human domination of other human beings. By this scientific analysis, he sought to develop a political knowledge base and pertinent political technology that could hand over the control of human domination—a mere fact of existence—to the most qualified person. Machiavelli looked to the history of human domination in order to retrieve the mechanisms that made domination feasible. Though Machiavelli "followed the events of his own time to the utmost degree of detail . . . he essentially saw himself as relying mostly upon history: side by side with the present, it is the past which must furnish the political scientist with examples from which he can detect regularities . . . the timeless rules by which people allow themselves to be dominated."[26]

Machiavelli shared with the natural sciences their metaphysical belief in the uniformity of events as well as in the uniformity of human nature. Proceeding from this belief, he refined a cyclical concept of the forms of government, in which the cycle of successive forms occurred with regularity, akin to a law of nature. Out of the convergence of scattered individuals emerged monarchy as the original form of government. As monarchy became monopolized through birth and degenerated into tyranny, aristocrats rebelled and set up an aristocratic regime. The aristocratic regime degenerated into oligarchic tyranny, which inevitably despised civil rights. The downfall of oligarchy ushered in a republican and even democratic form of government, and the latter eventually would turn anarchic. Only a strong dictator could rescue the situation, and only then could the cycle start anew.[27]

Horkheimer argues that Machiavelli advocated a powerful, "Machiavellian" ruler in order to stabilize the emerging bourgeois society in which Machiavelli lived. Only a forceful and, thus, stable state could provide the conditions that allow individual virtue to thrive. Furthermore, Machiavelli tied his notion of virtue to efficiency in business and industry, that is, to the adventuresome unfolding of free trade and economic powers. A virtuous government would be the stable, "Machiavellian" government. He promoted the absolutist state as the indispensable condition for the emergence of the possessive, bourgeois individual. No one, thought Machiavelli, can prevent the lawlike cycle of governmental forms. Still, like the natural scientist, the political scientist can learn the mechanisms well enough in order to intervene and, thus, to prolong a particular era.

According to Machiavelli, the exercise of power as domination depended on understanding the psychic mechanisms that determine human agency. Horkheimer explains that "for Machiavelli the characters of human beings constitute the ultimate explanatory material of the course of history, because they are composed of undeviating psychic elements, of eternally fixed instincts and passions."[28] "All men," said Machiavelli, ". . . are born and live and die in the same way, and therefore resemble each other."[29] Without this assumption, his "science" would have been a dream. By focusing on the biological factors of human nature as the driving force of history, Machiavelli anticipated by a century Descartes's alertness to bodies and the eventual empiricist fixation on bodies as the only factor worth investigating. Horkheimer argues that Machiavelli initiated the hypostatizing of the atomistic individual and thus "the bourgeois philosophy of history," though he "never moved beyond a naive understanding of the analogy between politics and physics, between the modes of explanation of natural science and of history."[30]

Hobbes, more consciously than Machiavelli, took up the theoretical analysis of the analogy between nature and human nature, between bodies and society, between physical systems under the mechanistic doctrine of nature and the union of human beings in a nation-state. Like the natural sciences, which had removed "God" as the determining factor for the understanding of natural causation, Hobbes removed God from social causation. Horkheimer cites Hobbes's mechanistic model of the state:

> For as in a watch, or some such small engine, the matter, figure, and motion of the wheels, cannot well be known, except it be taken in sunder, and viewed in parts; so to make a more curious search into the rights of States, and duties of Subjects, it is necessary, (I say not to take them in sunder, but yet that) they be so considered . . . .[31]

As an apologist for the absolutist state of his day, Hobbes did not analyze the course of world history. Rather, he conducted a thought-experiment. How would individuals act in the absence of a state, that is, in a state of nature? Horkheimer summarizes Hobbes:

> [S]ince human beings [being bodies] are only motivated either by pleasure or aversion, then life must be the highest good, and death the greatest evil. In the state of nature, the life of the individual is highly precarious. Although each person has a natural right to

everything in such a state of lawlessness, one must also continually expect to be robbed of everything by someone stronger, or occasionally even by someone who is weaker. Indeed, it is even possible for the weaker person to rob the stronger of the highest good, i.e., of life. . . . The state of nature is characterized by the boundless appetite of the individual—as well as the individual's fear of everyone else. The "*bellum omnium in omnes*" [the war of all against all] reigns supreme. From such fear arises the need for security, and from the latter arises the willingness to forego unlimited (and continually threatened) freedom. And so the social contract arises out of horror and hope, a compromise between our boundless aggression and our boundless anxiety.[32]

Here we have Hobbes's new concept of the "natural law" of self-preservation at the cost of unlimited freedom. In the state of nature, individuals contract with each other to transfer their authority to one person or assembly. Once the unlimited will of individuals is transferred to the state, only the will of the state is authoritative. The state fulfills its side of the contract by establishing the conditions that allow individuals to pursue the material bases of their self-preservation, that is, to pursue economic objectives, so long as no individual denies others the opportunity to do likewise.

In order to fulfill its contractual obligations, the state, according to Hobbes, takes on the nature of a great machine. Horkheimer continues:

Hobbes develops here the analogy from natural philosophy between the state, whose source is convention, and mathematical concepts, which are established by convention. . . . To contravene definitions in geometry is to commit an error; to contravene the laws of the state is to be a criminal or a rebel. Geometrical conventions were ultimately established in order to build machines; likewise, the convention of the original contract was arrived at in order to erect the greatest machine of all: the state. The function of this gigantic machine is to hold at bay the horror and anarchy of the original condition, to keep down all the monsters capable of endangering civil peace and security, above all the "behemoth": the monster of rebellion. Yet in truth, the state itself is none other than the most powerful monster, the "leviathan": the "mortal god" that governs as it pleases, and before whom the will of all other mortals keeps dumb.[33]

According to Hobbes, the social contract, culminating in statist authority, originated from the reasonableness of self-preservation. As Horkheimer sees it, the conjunction of individual self-preservation and reason lies at the heart of the bourgeois philosophy of history and eventually of "the [social] structure of the bourgeois order."

The social whole exists through unleashing the possessive instincts of all individuals. The whole is maintained insofar as individuals concern themselves with profit and with the conservation and multiplication of their own property. Each is left to care for himself as best as he can. But because, in the process, each individual must produce things that others need, the needs of the community as a whole end up being addressed through activities that are apparently independent of one another and seem only to serve the individual's welfare. That production and maintenance in this order coincide with the subjects' striving after possessions has left its impression on the psychic apparatus of community members. Throughout history, people have accommodated themselves in their entire being to the conditions of society; a consequence of this accommodation in the modern period is that human powers orient themselves to promoting individual advantage. This life-dominating principle leaves its mark on the individual's feelings, consciousness, form of happiness, and conception of God. Even in the individual's most refined and seemingly most remote impulses, the function he performs in society still makes itself felt. In the modern era, economic advantage is the natural law under which individual life proceeds.[34]

As Horkheimer sees it, Hobbes, at the pinnacle of the bourgeois philosophy of history, combined a new concept of natural law as rational, individual self-preservation with the machinelike nature of the state. In addition, this combination converged with empiricism to inaugurate a new and powerful social order within Western history: bourgeois, possessive individualism within an absolutist state, steered by an empiricist social science that would bring the preestablished mechanistic harmony of bourgeois interests to the surface. Horkheimer refers to this hybrid development as "traditional theory."

Toward "Critical" Theory

Horkheimer aims to overcome "traditional theory," with its destructive combination of epistemological empiricism and bourgeois atomistic individualism, by developing a "critical theory" of society. He begins this journey by probing the previous critics of traditional theory, beginning with Immanuel Kant's critical philosophy.

Agreements and Disagreements with Kant

Kant described his own critical philosophy as a "Copernican revolution" against the Cartesian rationalism still reigning in the late eighteenth century. As a student, Kant had been schooled in rationalism's concept of "pure" reason culminating in "certain" knowledge, untainted by fickle bodily sensation and experience. In fact, confessed Kant, he had been so certain of rationalism that he was in a "dogmatic slumber." He woke from his rationalist slumbers by reading Hume's empiricism, with its elevation of sense experience. Still, despite his own "critique of pure reason," Kant did not side with empiricism and its own insistence on "just the facts."

Horkheimer admires Kant's repudiation of "the adoration of facts and the social conformism this brings with it."[35] As usual, Horkheimer searches out the "real-life" stakes in the arcane epistemological feuds. Remember that empiricism, in a reversal of Descartes's dualistic elevation of mind and its productive reason, had reduced the mind to a blank slate and, thereby, had eliminated the human subject from any role, or, at least, from any *constructive* or *productive* role, in knowledge. Accordingly, human subjects, like minds, conformed to brute facts, or so empiricism surmised. Kant's epistemology, however, pointed in a different direction.

Against empiricism's dissolution of reason and the human subject, Kant planned to save both by delineating their proper limits. Descartes had failed to recognize these limits because he searched anxiously for absolute certainty and because he located this certainty in the subject's innate "I think."[36] Kant sought a solution by investigating the alliance between the passive sensation of experienced data and the active power of reason to organize sense data into a meaningful and truthful picture of reality, that is, by producing "knowledge." Horkheimer thinks that Kant was right to reclaim the human subject from the passive position to which empiricism had relegated it and to restore reason's contribution to the formation of knowledge. Critical theory, Horkheimer writes, must retrieve the vitality of the human subject and its productive reason if the reigning social "facticity" is not to have its way in the "real life" of German society and, indeed, in Western society more generally.[37]

Despite the gain that Kant represented vis-à-vis empiricism, Horkheimer finds Kant's epistemology flawed. Kant knew that the combination of passive sensation and active reason only begs a further question. From whence does reason gain its assurance to expect that the plethora of given sense data will always obey reason's organizing rules? Kant postulated that reason must depend on a "transcendental" realm of consciousness-in-itself—on a supra-individual, purely intellectual realm. Supplementing this postulation, Kant admitted that such a realm is "concealed in the depths of the human soul, whose real modes of activity nature is hardly likely ever to allow us to discover, and to have open to our gaze."[38]

Horkheimer agrees that there is some truth regarding the obscurity of knowledge's origin. Still, he is unsatisfied with Kant's mystification and agnosticism regarding the human subject's knowledge of the world. He argues that Kant's conceptualization of human knowing mirrors and, indeed, reinforces the dominant forms of heightened atomistic individuality that Horkheimer calls "bourgeois."

Bourgeois thought, in reflecting on the subject that exercises such thought, is forced by logical necessity to recognize an ego that imagines itself autonomous. Bourgeois thought is essentially abstract, and its principal characteristic is an individuality that believes itself to be the ground of the world, or even to be the world, without qualification, an individuality separated from events.[39] In this way Kant is the offspring of Descartes.[40]

Horkheimer's critical theory, by contrast, locates the "whence" of the individual's knowledge in real history and actual societies rather than in Kant's suprahistorical, asocial, transcendental "whence." Horkheimer finds important insights regarding the "whence" of knowledge in Hegel and Marx. Before pursuing those insights, however, I turn to Horkheimer's analysis of Kant's moral theory.

Kant's moral theory, according to Horkheimer, was connected in an odd way to the contemporary bourgeois society. Kant was aware that in a bourgeois society individuals conform to the so-called natural law of self-preservation. Following this natural law of self-preservation means that individuals pursue their own interest in happiness and seek, above all else, to possess the means for acquiring happiness. Morality, according to Kant, is set over and against this bourgeois version of self-preservation.

Kant formulated the moral point of view according to what he called "the categorical imperative," so named because the imperative, according to his thinking, is in a category or class by itself. The categorical imperative is superior to all other imperatives in that it is unconditionally binding, while others are binding only with certain conditions or in order to achieve certain useful ends. The categorical imperative is binding "no matter what." Kant stated the categorical imperative as follows: an individual must "act only according to that maxim by which you can at the same time will that it should become a universal law."

In light of the categorical imperative, "morality" is action that renounces one's individual interests or happiness—though these have their place—in favor of universal interests. Kant thereby prioritized "duty" to the social whole over the individual's self-preserving interest in happiness. Horkheimer notes that Kant, with his proposal for "the moral point of view," ostensibly recognized that the bourgeois structure of life did not accomplish what it claimed, that is, the public commonwealth through pursuit of private self-interest. Rather,

> the individual, completely absorbed in the concern for himself and "his own," does not only promote the life of the whole without clear consciousness; rather, he effects through his labor both the welfare and the misery of others—and it can never become entirely evident to what extent and for which individuals his labor means the one or the other. No unambiguous connection can be drawn between one's own labor and larger social considerations.[41]

Horkheimer's disagreement with Kant extends in another direction as well. The categorical imperative focused on the directive to be true to oneself and to have a moral will without self-contradiction. Kant, however,

> fails to provide a guiding rule that could remove the basis of moral uneasiness. Is there no misdeed that has been committed at some time or other in all good conscience? What is decisive for the happiness of humanity is not whether the individuals consider their action to be reconcilable with the natural law of the general welfare, but rather the extent to which it is actually reconcilable with it. Both the belief that a good will—as important an impulse as this may be—is the sole Good, and the evaluation of an action merely according to its intent and not also according to its real significance at a particular historical moment, amount to idealist delusions. From the ideological side of the Kantian conception of morality, a direct path leads to the modern mysticism of sacrifice and obedience, a mysticism which can only unjustly lay any further claim to the authority of Kant. . . . To be sure, the inner life of the acting individual is necessary for the very determination of both object and situation, for the internal and the external are every bit as much moments of manifold dialectical processes in all of history as they are in the life of the individual. But the prevalent

tendency in bourgeois morality to lay exclusive value upon conviction [i.e., one's intention] proves to be a position that inhibits
progress, especially in the present. . . . A will that is prepared to
make sacrifices may well be a useful resource in the service of any
power, including the most reactionary; insight into the relation in
which the will's content stands to the development of the entire
society, however, is given not by conscience but by the correct theory [of what is socially good].[42]

Kant's notion of the moral point of view ostensively recognized that "the
mode of action informed by the natural law of economic advantage is not
necessarily the rational mode."[43] Ironically, because his version of morality
presupposed the naturalness of the bourgeois way of life, it became "a consummate expression of its age."[44] Horkheimer is grateful, on the one hand,
for Kant's tacit recognition of the irrationality and immorality of the bourgeois way of life. On the other hand, he is distressed with the inability of
Kant's moral theory to abolish the bourgeois philosophy of history. Kant
merely compensated. Kant's moral theory collapses back upon itself
because it contains nothing more than a progressive concept of history, in
which individual and general interests eventually match. "The harmony of
the interests of all in Kant's utopia can only be understood as a pre-stabi-
lized harmony, as a charitable miracle."[45] Horkheimer sees the need for a
very different conceptualization of history, and this difference with Kant
will also have relevance for the concept of reason. He turns to Hegel's conceptualization of history as a beginning.

Agreements and Disagreements with Hegel

The road beyond Kant begins with Hegel. As Horkheimer sees it, Kant was
right to save human subjectivity from its demise at the hands of Hume's
skeptical empiricism. Kant believed that, when it comes to knowledge of
the world, the human subject possesses a productive mind that actively
contributes to the content of knowledge. Human subjectivity again was
wounded, however, because Kant in effect removed real subjectivity from
the realm of history and society and placed it in a transcendental domain
beyond time and space. Subjectivity and reason were disembodied, so to
speak.

Enter Hegel, who believed that the human subject and thus human
knowledge exist as a thoroughgoing historical process. Knowledge of the
world remains the knowledge of subjects embedded in historical contexts

and in human social interests. This represents one way that Hegel departed from Kant. Whereas Kant proposed to discover the human contribution to knowledge by probing a transcendental subject supposedly outside of time and space, Hegel rejected this notion of subjectivity. Horkheimer joins Hegel in "opposing the idea of an absolute, suprahistorical subject or the possibility of exchanging subjects, as though a person could remove himself from his present historical juncture and truly insert himself into any other he wished."[46] Hegel proposed to discover the human contribution to knowledge by probing the historical and social path that human knowers have traversed. Horkheimer's critical theory exploits this insight. The human knower "is rather a definite individual in his real relation to other individuals and groups, in his conflict with a particular class, and, finally, in the resultant web of relationships with the social totality and with nature."[47]

Knowledge, reason, and, indeed, truth itself entail a historical, social process.

> The objects we perceive in our surroundings—cities, villages, fields, and woods—bear the mark of having been worked on by man. It is not only in clothing and appearance, in outward form and emotional make-up that men are the product of history. Even the way they see and hear is inseparable from the social life-process as it has evolved over the millennia. The facts which our senses present to us are socially performed in two ways: through the historical character of the object perceived and through the historical character of the perceiving organ.[48]

And, again:

> Having confidence in rigorous, conscientious thinking on the one hand, and being aware of the conditionedness of the content and structure of cognitions on the other—far from being mutually exclusive, both attitudes are necessarily of a piece. The fact that reason can never be certain of its perpetuity; or that knowledge is secure within a given time frame, yet is never so for all time; or even the fact that the stipulation of temporal contingency applies to the very body of knowledge from which it is derived—this paradox does not annul the truth of the claim itself. Rather, it is of the very essence of authentic knowledge never to be settled once and for all. This is perhaps the most profound insight of all dialectical philosophy.[49]

The significance of social conflict represents the second key insight that Horkheimer takes from Hegel, thereby distinguishing a critical theory of society from traditional theory. Traditional theory embodied the positivistic notion of an inevitable, smoothly transpiring historical progress in which everyday, in every way, life is getting better. Hegel perceived history differently. He noted that at the eye of history lay a whirlwind of social contradiction and struggle. Herein lay Hegel's concept of historical dialectic and determinate negation. Every body of knowledge, that is, every truth, and every social embodiment of knowledge—a *thesis,* in Hegel's terminology—remains conditional and partial. Therefore, we can expect knowledge and its embodiment in a social organization to struggle with an opposing body of knowledge and its social embodiment—an *antithesis.* Still, this antithetical negation of the original body of knowledge and its social embodiment is not, as might be expected, rejection of the original. Rather, the antithesis deepens the partial knowledge and unfinished social embodiment of the original. This deepening leads to incorporating the partial truths of the thesis into the antithesis, and this incorporation gives birth to a new body of knowledge and its social embodiment—the *synthesis.*[50] In this way, history proceeds along the dialectical path of social struggle.

Horkheimer, like countless others before and after him, notes that Hegel did not escape from the tendency that Hegel had criticized in Kant and in German *idealism* in general. Hegel succumbed to the idealist retreat to an ahistorical domain beyond the messiness of historical struggle and contradiction. He did this in two related ways. First, he viewed his philosophical understanding of the historical dialectic as the final word. In effect, he perceived his own body of knowledge as absolute, as the whole truth, so to speak, and thereby beyond critique. As Horkheimer notes, Hegel's philosophy of history "is also marked by its hypostatization of conceptual structures and by the inability to take theoretical and practical account of the dogmatism and historical genesis of his own thought."[51] Second, Hegel viewed the Prussian state as the social embodiment of his own knowledge and, thereby, elevated it to the pinnacle of social-historical progress. Hegel's thought had come to conceal concrete misery and social suffering under his own glorious categories.

Agreements and Disagreements with Marx

Horkheimer harbors numerous agreements with Marx that Marx already had with Hegel. The most important areas of agreement for our purposes are the historical and social embeddedness of reason, knowledge, and truth and the process of historical dialectic. "Materialism [Marx's theory] obviously does not reject thinking. . . . But materialism, unlike idealism [even Hegel's], always understands thinking to be the thinking of particular men within a particular period of time."[52]

As a second point of agreement, Horkheimer concurs with Marx's materialist inversion of Hegel's dialectical idealism. That is, while Hegel viewed knowledge—ideas—as leading progress in history, Horkheimer, with Marx, sees "the fundamental historical role of economic relations" as the leader, thus Horkheimer and Marx's materialism.[53] In addition, their shared materialism "opposes every attempt to reduce social problems to second place . . . [which would merely] devalue the importance of providing proper economic foundations for society."[54] In this way, Horkheimer shares with Marx a focus on suffering and oppression lodged in the economic relations between owners of the means of production and workers.[55]

> [T]he critical theory of society is, in its totality, the unfolding of a single existential judgment. To put it in broad terms, the theory says that the basic form of the historically given commodity economy on which modern history rests contains in itself the internal and external tensions of the modern era; it generates these tensions over and over again in an increasingly heightened form; and after a period of progress, development of human powers, and emancipation for the individual, after an enormous extension of human control over nature, it finally hinders further development and drives humanity into a new barbarism.[56]

Following Marx in a third way, Horkheimer employs the concept of *ideology* and undertakes a critique. The notion of ideology combines the first two areas of agreement between Horkheimer and Marx. One's ideas are closely tied to one's historical and social situation, and one's historical and social situation is embedded in the economic relationships among and interests of different economic classes. That is, ideas—systems of ideas—and their "rationality" cleave to and, indeed, comply with the economic interests of the powerful. In ideology there is "something of an alliance between truth and ascending classes."[57] Ideology consists of the economically interested rationale of those who own the means of production, the moneyed class. A critique of ideology demands analysis of this cartel of reason—understood as rationale—and economic interest.[58] When the moneyed class promotes class inequality as the rational way of the world, they employ ideology. When they do so with a good conscience, they suffer "false consciousness," "self-deception," and "ignorance." When they do so knowingly, they practice "cunning," "the will to dominate," and idolatry. When the working class accedes "knowingly and willingly" to ideology, they practice false consciousness as well. When they simply capitulate, they submit to "irrationality" and the opiate of "myth."[59] "After Marx, we are forbidden any such consolation [on the basis of some idealist or religious paradise or of any purely intellectual order] about the world."[60] In chapter 3 I examine Horkheimer's understanding of *critique* in "the critique of ideology." His understanding appears under the term *immanent critique.*

Finally, Horkheimer adopts Marx's accent on the significance of practice, agents, and agency.[61] Indeed, Horkheimer agrees that the focus must be on emancipatory practice and agents and, finally, on emancipatory politics.[62] But here we discover Horkheimer's departure from Marx and his basis for ceasing to call his theory "materialism" or *Marxism.*

Marx thought that the proletariat would be the revolutionary, emancipatory agents for transforming capitalist society. In fact, he claimed that this was predictable based on a calculable, historical determinism. Horkheimer, by contrast, was witnessing large segments of the proletariat in Germany enthusiastically embracing fascism. As he notes, "[E]ven the situation of the proletariat is, in this society, no guarantee of correct knowledge."[63]

This situation leads Horkheimer and his "critical theory of society" in a different direction from Marxism, and this would eventually arouse extensive criticism from orthodox Marxists.[64] Horkheimer starts looking for a different emancipatory agent than the proletariat. He finds it, at least in part, in emancipatory intellectuals, in theorists like himself, and in the kind of researchers that he assembles at the Institute of Social Research. Horkheimer must consider how theory is not only critical but also how it constitutes an emancipatory practice. From this time forward, the relationship of theory and practice, specifically political practice, remains a core consideration of the critical theory of society. "[T]he first consequence of the theory which urges a transformation of society as a whole is only an intensification of the struggle with which the theory is connected."[65] Moreover, "[t]he hostility to theory as such which prevails in contemporary public life is really directed against the transformative activity associated with critical thinking."[66] This ennobling of theory and theoreticians departs from Marx and presents problems that we discuss in chapter 3.

By directly criticizing Marx's deterministic theory, Horkheimer again highlights "the essential relatedness of theory to time."[67] Here we have another core component of Horkheimer's idea of critical social theory. "The historical development of the conflicts in which critical theory is involved leads to a reassignment of degrees of relative importance to individual elements of the theory, forces further concretizations, and determines which results of specialized science are to be significant for critical theory and practice at any given time."[68] In fact, according to critical theory the "influence of social development on the structure of the theory is part of the theory's doctrinal content."[69] This "doctrine" means that critical theory might analyze factors that Marxist materialism considered impertinent, like art, culture, personality, and others. New factors also require, in addition to Marxist economic analysis, new disciplines.

We have now come full circle, to the hybrid nature of critical social theory and to Horkheimer's idea for the Institute of Social Research. We will find this enduring "doctrine" of critical social theory a crucial reason that Habermas moves in his thinking along the paths of the communicative imagination and deliberative democracy. Such new developments also warrant new reflections regarding the prophetic imagination, and they contribute to my proposal for a communicative prophetic imagination within a civil society poised with political purpose.

The relation between theory and time means "the theory as a whole is caught up in an evolution."[70] Neither social development nor the evolution of theory, however, indicates a progressive philosophy of history on Horkheimer's part or in critical theory as a whole. "[A] return to barbarism is always open."[71] In chapter 3, I probe where social developments of the 1940s take Horkheimer's critical social theory and how this evolution leads him, ironically, toward a devolutionary philosophy of history.

2

Tillich: Christian Engagement with Critical Social Theory

The association between critical social theory and Christian theology goes back to the beginning of Horkheimer's appointment as the director of the University of Frankfurt's Institute of Social Research. At the time—1929—when the fledgling institute was searching for a new director, Paul Tillich was a professor of philosophy at the university.[1] Tillich pushed hard for the appointment of Horkheimer as director. In the few years between Horkheimer's appointment and his and Tillich's forced departure from the university and from Germany under pressure from the Nazi government, Tillich was an active participant within the circle that Horkheimer drew into the institute's orbit. In fact, Tillich was fondly referred to by institute members as "Paulus [St. Paul] among the Jews."[2] Further, Tillich and Horkheimer offered three joint seminars on philosophy from 1930–31.[3]

We proceed in this chapter in five stages. First, we enter an interpretive conflict about Tillich's association with critical social theory.[4] Second, we review how Tillich directly engages the tradition of critical social theory. Third, we investigate how Tillich, within his theological engagement with critical social theory, explores the relationship between reason and the prophetic imagination. Fourth, we explore the relationship between the form of grace and the Protestant congregation. Finally, I critically assess Tillich's understanding of the prophetic imagination. This assessment will help us see how the ongoing development of critical social theory continues to be a worthy companion of Christian prophetic imagination.

An Interpretive Conflict

In a 1984 collection of essays, Terrence O'Keeffe observed that "[a] number of recent commentators on Paul Tillich's social and political thought

have drawn attention to links between Tillich and the Frankfurt School."[5]
O'Keeffe singled out Ronald Stone's 1977 article in the *Union Seminary Quarterly Review,* in which Stone noted that Tillich "was closely associated with" the members of the Institute of Social Research. Stone argued that a right "understanding of his [Tillich's] social philosophy" would emerge only if placed within the social context of the institute.[6]

Stone aspired already in 1977 to position Tillich as a "radical political theologian."[7] During the 1970s, the meaning of "political theology" became important along with its relation to the burgeoning liberation theologies of Latin America, Africa, Asia, and North America. Stone was combating an interpretive trend at Union Seminary in New York, among other places, that viewed Tillich as having, increasingly over his life, become an apolitical theologian. According to this viewpoint, Tillich's great influence in North America meant that he had given too much North American theology an apolitical interpretation.

Stone countered this interpretive trend by borrowing an insight from the sociology of knowledge. Ideas, Tillich's as well, are social products rather than notions that spring from nowhere. "Tillich's social theory was always a social product. He worked his ideas out in discussion and he wrote in loyalty to those with whom he talked." Tillich's association with the Frankfurt School "indicates the type of social theory and research that interested" him. Stone hoped to save Tillich from dispatch to Union Seminary's garbage heap for apolitical theologians. "Therefore, the placing of some of Tillich's ideas in the social context of the thinking of the Institut für Sozialforschung [Institute of Social Research] at the University of Frankfort helps in explaining several important developments in Tillich's thought." Stone knew that Union Seminary in New York held the Frankfurt School in high regard, and he offered his audience a new "avenue for understanding the Germanic origins of this immigrant's philosophy of culture and religion and its impact upon North America."[8]

Stone's interpretive conflict with Union Seminary stimulated O'Keeffe to examine and to refute the putative links between Tillich and the Frankfurt School. Likewise, O'Keeffe's dispute with Stone stirred yet another disputant, James Champion. I engage Champion's interpretation of Tillich's relation with critical social theory, because Champion raised crucial issues for the ongoing encounter between critical social theory and Christian theology and, finally, for a contemporary inquiry into the prophetic imagination.

O'Keeffe's query to Stone's interpretive proposal runs: "Do the links that can be established enable us to talk about an interdependence between Tillich's socialist thought and the Critical Theory of the institute, of a mutual influence and a shared perspective between the Frankfurt School and the Marxism of Tillich?"[9] O'Keeffe contests the "mutual influence" theory by refuting a suggestion Martin Jay made in his highly regarded account of the Frankfurt School. Jay had stated that the biographical link marking the institute's members was their Jewishness.[10] Contrary to Jay's suggestion, O'Keeffe argues that their common commitment to Marxism bound institute members. Further, they all had a common enemy in how Marx was to be interpreted. That is, they rejected Lenin's then-ascendant "orthodox" version of scientific Marxism.[11] O'Keeffe focuses on the institute's Marxism and its goal of a Marxism "better understood." This enhances consideration of a mutual influence between Tillich and the institute, since Tillich too sought a Marxism better understood. O'Keeffe, in fact, uses the first twelve pages of his twenty-page analysis to explore the neo-Marxism that Tillich and the Frankfurt School, in theory, had in common. In these pages, O'Keeffe adds ten reasons to Stone's fivefold account of mutual influence, all of which might "suggest that we can speak of definite links, mutual influence, even interdependence of ideas." "But," O'Keeffe continues, "several points militate against this immediate conclusion."[12]

While the mutual-influence theory appears plausible initially, it does not finally persuade him. He cites four critical differences between Tillich and the Frankfurt School that lead one to conclude a "lack of mutual influence."[13] The first factor, though not the weightiest, is "the almost total ignorance of each other's writings at the scholarly level."[14] Second, O'Keeffe mentions that Tillich "constantly sought to incorporate religion into socialist theory . . . to [quoting Tillich's own words] 'overcome the static opposition of the concepts of religion and socialism by demonstrating their dialectical relationship.'" In contrast to Tillich, the religion factor, in O'Keeffe's telling, is "a strand of thought conspicuously lacking in the Critical Theory of this period." O'Keeffe disputes Jay's interpretation concerning the bond that Jewishness gave the institute's members, specifically because religion possesses no gravity in the institute's work at the time, though it enters some of the members' theories at later times. O'Keeffe does not dwell long on the religion factor as he builds his "lack of mutual influence" case. Rather, he eagerly pursues a third factor that, as he sees it, accounts for the lack of mutual influence. In my view, religion does represent a weighty element in this initial engagement between critical social theory and Christian theology. I inquire more deeply into the religion factor after reviewing briefly why O'Keeffe desires to restrict altogether the role that religion might play in the relation between Tillich and critical social theory.

O'Keeffe trivializes religion as a possible difference because his third factor singlehandedly warrants the thesis that Tillich and the Frankfurt School did not depend on each other's work. In O'Keeffe's argument, the consequential difference between Tillich and the institute resides in the interpretation of Marxist theory. While both Tillich and the institute rejected a Leninist, "scientific" interpretation of Marxism, they differed in the positive interpretive direction that they sought to take Marxist theory and practice. As O'Keeffe sees it, the institute's members focused on commodity exchange as the key for understanding Marx's analysis of society. Tillich, notes O'Keeffe, perceived the true significance of Marx's analysis to lie in the loss of meaning experienced in the proletariat and located in its alienated and reified social status.[15] On the basis of his first three warrants, heavily weighted toward the third, O'Keeffe postulates "a definite conclusion. . . . [D]espite the many parallels we have noted, these remain only parallels. We conclude that Tillich's socialism developed more or less independently of the thought of the Institute for Social Research. Despite the many ties of friendship with all the leading figures in critical theory, and despite a community of interests and preoccupations, there was little, if any, mutual influence."[16]

Curiously, O'Keeffe does not conclude his account on this note. On the contrary, he skillfully continues his analysis for four more pages by drawing from the discussion of Marxist theory the "final" and, for O'Keeffe, the clinching warrant for his noninfluence thesis. His final point regards real-life political practice and the nexus between theory and praxis. "[T]he real difference between Tillich and the Frankfurt School lay in their respective attitudes toward the actual political situation of the 1930s and during the war. . . . [T]he Frankfurt School failed to make the link between theory and genuine political action. . . . Tillich was different. . . . He . . . sought 'an active participation in politics during the last years of Weimar, an attitude Tillich maintained at least up to the late '40s.'"[17] Horkheimer's and Adorno's "negative pessimism" decisively distinguished them from Tillich's "political realism and activism."[18] O'Keeffe regrets, however, that by the end of the 1940s Tillich, too, had withdrawn from political life. In the case of Horkheimer and Adorno, O'Keeffe agrees that they fell into "the reduction of politics to philosophy."[19] While registering admiration for Tillich for attempting a socialist political stance during the general collapse of working-class movements, O'Keeffe finally renders the same judgment on Tillich. Tillich notoriously attained "the reduction of politics to theology." O'Keeffe credits this fateful reduction to "the almost totally" apolitical text of Tillich's *Systematic Theology*. In my estimation, O'Keeffe's thoroughgoing rejection of the post-1940s Tillich lacks the nuance necessary for a Tillich "better understood." O'Keeffe flounders because he trivializes the religion factor for Tillich—as well as for Horkheimer—while Tillich addressed real social and political practice in the 1920s, 1930s, and 1940s. We must now explore this "religion" factor. Our interest will not be confirming or rejecting some form of the mutual-influence thesis. Rather, Tillich's understanding of *religious* socialism will help gain preliminary clarity about the Christian prophetic imagination.

Champion's interpretation in "Tillich and the Frankfurt School" will help our discussion in three ways. First, Champion directly refutes O'Keeffe's bifurcationist interpretation of an early, political Tillich contrasted with a late, apolitical Tillich. Second, Champion focuses on the religion factor in reference both to Tillich and to Horkheimer and Adorno. Third, Champion highlights the prophetic imagination—as we are calling it—as the salient religious element. He thematizes this last point with the essay's subtitle, "Parallels and Differences in Prophetic Criticism." For our purposes, we forgo Champion's argument against a bifurcationist interpretation of Tillich, though I tend to agree with its thrust. Champion enters the discussion regarding the "Jewishness" of the institute's members in order to frame his inquiry into the prophetic factor and to state his thesis regarding "their common movement beyond rational criticism of culture and society to engage in prophetic critique."[20] My divergence from Champion's interpretation of the "parallels and differences in prophetic criticism" between Tillich, on the one hand, and Horkheimer and Adorno, on the other, turns on how Champion frames what they hold in common. As Champion frames—misframes—his inquiry, they share a movement *beyond* rational criticism *to* prophetic critique, as if prophetic critique leaves rational criticism behind. Our investigation into the characteristics of rational criticism and prophetic critique and into how Tillich, then Horkheimer and Adorno, construe the relationship between the two ideas will contribute significantly to our exploration of Christian prophetic imagination.

Champion pursues the religion factor in the Frankfurt School in order to overcome O'Keeffe's denial that "Jewishness" was significant for critical social theory. O'Keeffe, as we saw, denies the significance of Jewishness in order to undermine Stone's mutual-influence thesis. Champion endorses the mutual-influence thesis, and this strengthens the perception of Tillich as a thoroughly political theologian. I favor the mutual-influence opinion, although I doubt that enough indisputable evidence exists to support it unambiguously. Still, I think that Martin Jay's initial hunch is on target. The Jewishness of the institute's members did influence at least the initial quest, in the late 1920s and early 1930s, for a *critical* social theory, and their religiousness may have guided key members in the 1940s. According to Jay's account, the Jewish refusal to name and, thus, to pin down the deity—the sacred—became "one of the central premises of Critical Theory from the start."[21] Champion argues that O'Keeffe overlooks the Jewishness of critical social theory because he fails to acknowledge the common post-Enlightenment "scandal of theological survivals in even the most secular thinkers." In Champion's assessment, the Jewishness of the institute's members is largely covert, "a modern, thoroughly secularized version of the Jewish prophetic principle." Still, he writes, such covertness "does not diminish" the Jewish prophetic significance.[22]

Champion supports his position regarding the significant though covert Jewishness of Horkheimer and Adorno by comparing them to two other German-Jewish thinkers, Walter Benjamin and Ernst Bloch, with whom they had significant dialogue. Benjamin and Bloch exhibited a more "self-consciously Jewish and radical messianism" and thus more Jewish "overtness." Champion, however, overlooks a crucial point in his exposition of the religion factor. Because he identifies the covert-overt polarity as the crucial religious difference between Horkheimer and Adorno, on the one hand, and Benjamin and Bloch, on the other, he misses the weightier difference. This difference rests on the freestanding—covert, for sure—character of Horkheimer and Adorno's Jewish prophetism. For Horkheimer and Adorno, prophetism stands free from the historical legacy of Jewish redemptive messianism that both Benjamin and Bloch intentionally seek to combine with their overt Jewish prophetism.[23] Not surprisingly, Champion then employs covert-overt difference to interpret the commonality and difference between Horkheimer/Adorno and Tillich. In Champion's construal, while the prophetic is hidden and thus covert in Horkheimer and Adorno, it is "described" and thus overt in Tillich.[24] If we settled for this

TILLICK THR IS A NECESSARY

CONNECTION BTN RATIONAL CRITICISM & 33

PROPHETIC CRITIQUE

construal, we would miss Tillich's argument for the necessary connection between rational criticism and prophetic critique. This connection stands as the weightier difference between Tillich and Horkheimer/Adorno. Furthermore, this connection is the crucial reason for the Christian prophetic imagination to engage critical social theory vigorously. CHAMPION —

What does it mean that Horkheimer and Adorno move beyond rational criticism to prophetic critique? According to Champion's interpretation of prophetic critique, the very nature of prophetism means that its critique becomes total, even when exercised in the covert manner of Horkheimer and Adorno. In other words, prophetism, as Champion construes it, entails a total consignment of reason to the status of power, and to power in the sense of pure domination. Further, Champion ascribes this totalist trait to prophetism's "transcendent perspective," whether exercised covertly or overtly.[25] As we turn to Tillich's own formulation, we find that prophetism does not have to entail such totalism. The prophetic imagination does not pass beyond rational criticism as if *beyond* means abandoning rational criticism and consigning rationality in toto to the province of power as domination. Tillich's exposition is different. A "transcendent perspective," even when asserted overtly as Tillich does, does not relinquish or renounce rational criticism and thereby does not end with totalistic critique. Tillich's prophetic imagination entails a dynamic configuration, with each type of criticism making a contribution. Were we to follow Champion's framing of the religion factor, we would lose Tillich's insights into the Christian prophetic imagination and, specifically, into how critical social theory can be a public companion to that imagination and vice versa.

Engagement in Critical Reverence

A snapshot of Tillich's interpretation of the prophetic imagination, with specific reference to critical social theory, appears in his 1941 review of Herbert Marcuse's *Reason and Revolution*.[26] Marcuse, the most respected of the Frankfurt School members after Horkheimer and Adorno, interprets Hegel's philosophy in its social and political context as well as with reference to the social and political consequences that it had for the emerging situation in Europe. Tillich notes that Marcuse's book "constitutes a monumental introduction to the . . . socio-historical . . . method of 'critical theory' as developed by Max Horkheimer and his Institute for Social Research." Tillich approvingly underscores Marcuse's contention that Hegel's philosophy "[was] originally motivated by the conviction that the given facts that appear to common sense as the positive index of truth are in reality the negation of truth, so that truth can only be established by their [the given facts that appear to common sense] destruction. The driving force of the dialectical method is this critical conviction." Hegel's revolutionary notion of reason becomes "the bridge from Kant and the bourgeois revolution to Marx and the proletarian revolution, with critical dialectics serving as the main cable of that bridge."[27]

While Tillich "agrees in all important points" with Marcuse's proposed link between reason and revolution, he crafts two criticisms. The second criticism suggests that Marcuse's proposal would benefit from a nuanced distinction between types of positivism.[28] The first criticism goes to the heart of the engagement between critical social theory and the Christian imagination. Early in the review, Tillich diplomatically suggests that Marcuse's account of Hegel's philosophy "somewhat neglected" Hegel's interpretation of religion.[29] In the closing remarks, Tillich returns to this intentionally cordial understatement. Tillich, with his carefully chosen words, displays a critical reverence for at least two reasons. First, he and Marcuse had team-taught philosophy at the University of Frankfurt in the early 1930s, and, second, he was writing the review for the English-language journal of the then-exiled Institute of Social Research. Tillich argues: "Even a critical social theory cannot avoid an 'ultimate' in which its criticism is rooted because reason itself is rooted therein."[30] Notice that Tillich does not say "*should* not avoid," but rather, "*cannot*." There is an ontologically transcendent rootedness of reason that is real. Hegel knew this and argues for it. Tillich briefly lists the consequences of avoiding this reality.[31] Without an ultimate root for critical revolutionary reason, "criticism itself becomes positivistic and contingent."[32] By "positivistic," Tillich means "reactionary," and thus without convincing argument for the error and evil of a particular set of social and historical conditions. By "contingent," Tillich means a critical engagement too dependent on mere happenstance and thus lacking an obligatory edge and an ontologically enduring impulse or staying power. Without basis in an "ultimate," rational criticism runs into a wall, like marathoners at the twenty-mile marker. Only an ultimate ground can empower critical revolutionaries beyond critique fatigue. He incorporates such sentiments in the sentence immediately following his warning about positivism and contingency: "And no successful revolution can be made without a group of people who—however critical they may be of any special religious

TILLICH

symbol—believe that the 'freedom of personality' is the meaning of existence and are ready to live and die for this belief. The pervasive disappointment over the last revolutions demonstrates this irrefutably." Even though, admits Tillich, religion can function ideologically—that is, as false rationalization for passivity in the face of oppressive social situations (as Feuerbach argues) or for promotion of oppressive social arrangements (as Marx argues)—"it is a wrong generalization, derived from a metaphysical materialism, to dismiss religion itself as ideology." Tillich admonishes: "The transformation of philosophy [specifically Hegel's] into critical theory does not imply such a consequence at all." This condensed discussion of the relation of religion and critical social theory previews a more thorough consideration of the prophetic imagination. For this we turn to Tillich's pivotal, programmatic essay from 1929, "Protestantism as a Critical and Creative Principle."[33]

Rational Criticism and Prophetic Imagination

Tillich embarks on his investigation within Germany of the 1920s. He examines the emerging theological options and the implications of these options for engaging the historical situation. While certainly contextualized, Tillich's inquiry retains enduring significance because it distances itself by a half-step from the most immediate and concrete political and religious options available in Germany during the 1920s. That is, he intentionally selects an encompassing, retrospective point of view toward Protestantism over the previous century. Unbeknownst to Tillich, this point of view remains relevant for the middle and latter half of the twentieth century. At least two reasons come to mind. First, crises in the Christian prophetic imagination continue throughout the twentieth century. Second, Karl Barth's theological vision still exerts significant influence, a vision that Tillich engages in his essay.[34]

Tillich divulges the framework of his inquiry in his title. The essay's two parts are "Protestantism as a Critical Principle" and "Protestantism as a Creative and Formative Principle." Tillich divides the first part into two sections: "The Two Types of Criticism" and "Protestant Criticism." He does the same with the second part, dividing it into "The Two Kinds of Form-Creation" and "The Creative and Formative Powers of Protestantism." I concentrate on the essay's first part, though I review his second line of inquiry as well.

The Integrity of Rational and Prophetic Criticisms

Tillich points out that criticism of particular worldviews and of concrete social reality—what he calls intellectual and social forms—can proceed from two different points of view. The first point of view yields a type of criticism that he calls "rational criticism," and the second point of view yields what he calls "prophetic criticism." "Protestantism as a Critical Principle" analyzes the distinction between and the collaboration of these two types of criticism. By "rational criticism," Tillich means the variety of modern, critical disciplines for rationally analyzing cultural, psychological, sociological, and religious structures and conditions. He defines *rational* as "anything confined to or belonging intrinsically within the sphere of reason, anything connected with the formulation of concepts and 'ideal' constructions. An 'ideal' can, however, be acquired in a very irrational way, for example, intuitively."[35] As such rational criticism "is the standpoint of the ideal by which the particular form is measured . . . [it] presupposes a definite standpoint by means of which it is able to pronounce its Yes or its No. It is a rational procedure, even though [or when] the criterion itself has not been reached in a rational way." By "prophetic criticism," Tillich means "that which lies beyond the creation of form . . . [by which] form-creation as such is brought into question. . . . [Prophetic] criticism possesses no criterion at all; for that which lies beyond form-creation is not a form that can be used for the measurement of other forms. Therefore, it does not pronounce a Yes or a No, but combines an unconditional No with an unconditional Yes."[36]

Sensing the highly stylized and abstract nature of his remarks, Tillich offers three examples to clarify the difference between rational and prophetic criticism. "Thus, for example, any scientific result is measured by that standard of scientific evidence which is valid in the particular field in question." This exemplifies rational criticism. With prophetic criticism, however, "the structure of science as such is brought into question—and perhaps justified—by what is beyond all human knowledge, by what is 'higher than all reason.'"[37] Two other examples illustrate the distinction.

> Thus, [according to rational criticism] on the one hand, a social institution is measured by some social ideal, for example, justice in one or another of its various formulations. On the other hand, [according to prophetic criticism] the whole social organization as such is questioned—and perhaps justified—by what lies beyond all social organizations, by what is "boundless," as over against the

actual life of justice. Again, the ethical maturity of any man is, [according to rational criticism] on the one hand, measured by the ideal of ethical personality and his approximation to this ideal. On the other hand, [according to prophetic criticism] the ethical personality as such in its maturity or immaturity is brought into question—and perhaps justified—by "the holy" that lies beyond all personality.[38]

At this point, Tillich explores how the rational-prophetic distinction helps to overcome the conceptual cul-de-sacs that he encountered in the philosophy of *vitalism,* an emerging school of thought in early twentieth-century Germany. Among the conceptual quagmires were: What is criticism's source? From where do its standards and criteria come? Tillich continues, "Both kinds of criticism have their source in the act whereby man rises above mere being as such."[39] He has in mind precisely the kind of question at the crux of Horkheimer's inquiry about the pervasive givenness of the status quo. "Thus," continues Tillich, "both modes of criticism presuppose a break with immediacy of being." By "immediacy of being," he means the nontransparency of the reigning order—the overwhelming givenness, matter-of-factness, that's-just-the-way-it-isness of the status quo.[40]

A rough analogue from everyday life might help us grasp the immediacy-of-being problem with which Tillich wrestles. In college, Psychology 101 students learn about the "fight or flight" reflex. When caught in immediate and overwhelming danger, animals are seized by an instinctual reflex either to fight or run. Upon learning this as a student, I quickly recalled my grandmother's admonition to "count to ten" when faced with another's verbal abuse rather than reacting immediately with angry aggression. Through her proverbial, and persistent, wisdom, grandma was instilling in me a "second nature," a habitual practice that procures distance from the immediacy of my being, from the givenness or matter-of-factness of my fight reflex.[41] Counting to ten was a stepping back, a reflective and reflexive habit, or, and here is the analogy, a "break with immediacy."

While this break with immediacy is common to rational and prophetic criticism, "[t]he significance of this break, however, is different in each type." In rational criticism, "criticism remains within the sphere of being; what is immediately given is measured by true being, the 'given' is measured by what is sought after and also demanded." Ethics is the discipline for measuring the immediately given. This is why the criteria of rational criticism are "what is sought after and also demanded." "What is sought after" alludes to the heritage of teleological ethical reflection. The foremost question in the teleological heritage concerns the natural "goods" to be pursued, those that aid and result in the flourishing of human—and today we would include environmental—life. Tillich's "what is demanded" alludes to the heritage of deontological ethical reflection. The foremost question in the deontological heritage concerns the duties or obligations enjoined for the well-being of others. The conundrum or paradox of rational criticism is that "its starting point [is] in being and at the same time is directed against it [being]. Its presupposition is the bifurcation of being into that which is in conformity with its essence and that which is estranged from its essence."[42] Ethics refers to this paradox of rational criticism as the is-ought question.

Prophetic criticism is of a different sort from the ethically oriented character of rational criticism. Prophetic criticism "implies a transcending of existential being, whether it is in conformity with its essence or in opposition to it."[43] This difference, which we will explore in greater depth, is important to grasp. If we do not grasp the difference, we risk minimizing or losing the integrity and mission of both types of criticism. We also risk minimizing or losing their collaborative mission.

Before Tillich explores the integrity of each and the collaboration of both, he intentionally floats a premature conclusion. "The transcending of being," implied in the coming of prophetic criticism, "is faith." He provocatively introduces faith, because from the outset he wants to rout the Kantian captivity of prophetic criticism. This Kantian captivity, due to Albrecht Ritschl and his entourage, had gained increasing dominance over the previous fifty years. Since, Tillich continues, "[t]his transcending of being is 'faith,' [i]t is, therefore, absolutely contradictory to speak of a 'religion within.'" By "religion within," Tillich indicts Kant's construal of "religion within mere reason." Further, when Kant—and Albrecht Ritschl, who follows him—conceptualizes religion within the province of reason, he means practical or moral reason. The reduction of religion to morality, Kantian or otherwise, is Tillich's target at this point. Kant claims that his understanding of religion involves the act of transcending being. Tillich argues that Kant's claim is wrong. In Kant's construal, Tillich writes, "this act really remains within the sphere that should be transcended."[44] The Kantian captivity of religion had become the deep structure of the self-sufficient, autonomous culture that characterized Germany during the late nineteenth century and into the first decades of the twentieth century. Religion had been almost completely absorbed into German culture. The prophetic imagination had been colonized. The consequences for prophetic criticism were disastrous, though the road to disaster had been shrewdly camouflaged.

Where the Kantian captivity of religion "is predominant, prophetic criticism is inevitably identified with rational criticism and the unconditioned transcendent is confused with the conditioned transcendent of spirit."[45] Eventually, prophetic criticism dissolves into rational criticism.[46] In Tillich's assessment, nineteenth-century liberal, cultural Protestantism had descended to this point. He was not alone in this perception. Karl Barth's dialectical theology was born out of a similar appraisal. For Tillich, the reduction of prophetic criticism to rational criticism, brought on by Ritschlean liberal, cultural Protestantism, makes it incumbent for theology to inquire: "[H]ow far do both kinds of criticism follow the same path and where do they separate?"[47]

In order to respond decisively to this question, Tillich poses the following consideration: "[I]f the criticism that proceeds from what is beyond being and spirit is genuine criticism, that is, if it has the power of 'dividing,' then it must not proceed in such a way as to question being and spirit merely *in abstracto* [in abstraction]."[48] By this caveat, Tillich registers his difference with the Barthian school of dialectical theology of the 1920s. This difference arises despite their equal disdain for the prophetic collapse of Ritschlean Protestantism.[49] Tillich's analysis of dialectical theology hinges on a critique of "abstractly prophetic criticism."[50] Prophetic criticism *in abstracto* "would not lead to a real division (crisis), it would only leave everything as it was or, rather, it would leave concrete criticism—that is, effective criticism—to the rational approach. . . . [T]he relationship obtaining between the two kinds of criticism is not in this way adequately dealt with."[51] Tillich's point is that prophetic criticism, if abstracted from rational criticism, as in Barthian dialectical theology, leaves the status quo intact.

The Collaboration of Rational and Prophetic Criticisms

Until this point in his essay, Tillich has focused on the distinguishable integrity of rational and prophetic criticism. Now he seeks to assure that the distinction between the two types does not degenerate into a separation.

*Dialectical
Theology
is
effectural
critical
but only
in the
sphere of
Theology*

In our day we hear frequent reference to the "existential" character of prophetic criticism. It is well that our attention should have been directed to the significance of prophetic criticism and especially that the character of "unconditioned concern," which attaches to all religious proclamation, should have been emphasized. But the concreteness of prophetic criticism is not sufficiently expressed by this characterization alone. The decisive point is the way in which the term *existential* is interpreted. Prophetic criticism can become concrete only if the existential embraces the entire sphere of being, and in such a way that there is a "division" [a differentiation between unconditioned and conditioned] within it [the entire sphere of being]. Therefore the prophetic criticism of the Old Testament, the criterion of all genuinely prophetic criticism, always includes a concrete rational criticism.[52]

Tillich regarded dialectical theology as having been an effective prophetic criticism of the previous dominant theology. But its prophetic effectiveness had been limited to the sphere of theology.

> The effectiveness of dialectical theology was limited because it overlooked the indissoluble relationship between the theological ideal and all other ideals, and therefore of theological criticism and all other rational criticism; thus it unintentionally relegated everything having to do with theology to a separate domain of prophetic criticism. The effect of this was to weaken to some extent the religious criticism that had been directed against other cultural spheres, for example, the criticism that had been advanced by "religious socialism," and therefore to strengthen the existing forms and powers of secular life.[53]

Because dialectical theology's prophetic criticism had been abstract with regard to the intellectual disciplines of the university, it allowed these disciplines contentedly to preserve dominant forms of public life in Germany. This tendency also had an isolating effect on dialectical theology, so that the rational criticism of the other disciplines remained cut off from theology. Ironically, therefore, "abstract criticism exercised a conservative influence upon theology itself." Tillich laments, "The separation of the two types of criticism has, as this development shows, brought about a weakening of the critical attitude in general."[54]

Having diagnosed dialectical theology's sundering of the two types of criticism, Tillich attends to how prophetic and rational criticism "depend

CRITICISM IS GIVEN ITS 'EXISTENTIAL' CHARACTER (CONCRETENESS, INEVITABILITY, UNCONDITIONEDNESS) VIA COLLABORATION OF RATIONAL & PROPHETIC

upon each other."[55] "Prophetic criticism becomes concrete in rational criti- *CRITICISM* cism. On the other hand, rational criticism acquires from prophetic criti- cism the quality of inevitability and unconditionedness." Tillich goes on to stress that these three qualities—concreteness, inevitability, and uncondi- tionedness—in their collaboration give prophetic criticism its "existential" character. Further, rational criticism that lacks the prophetic characteristics of inevitability and unconditionedness will not be poignantly existential. Rational criticism by itself can "only strive to bring about an approxima- tion of 'resistant' existence to true being." Because rational criticism, by itself, lacks inevitability, it lacks "ultimate seriousness" or "depth."[56] That is, rational criticism, when standing free from prophetic criticism, cannot ade- quately address the fundamental question: why be moral in the first place?[57]

Tillich focuses on one more element in the dynamic collaboration between rational criticism and prophetic criticism. That rational criticism needs prophetic criticism's depth reveals "the limitations inherent within" rational criticism. *GRACE SUBJECTS PROPHETIC CRITICISM*

TO CRITICISM

The element in prophetic criticism that makes "being" problematic does not point to a fulfillment in the existential order. Rather, the fulfillment comes in a sphere beyond the critical situation. This is expressed in the word *grace*. Through grace, even prophetic criticism is subjected to criti- cism. Any ultimate right for prophetic criticism to negate and to go beyond being is denied. But this right is denied only after prophetic criticism has itself advanced to the stage of unconditioned seriousness.[58]

There is no doubt that Tillich is arguing for recognition of a crucial limit in rational criticism, and that this limit exists and is even intensified through the seriousness that rational criticism receives from prophetic crit- icism. At issue for Tillich seems to be whether rational criticism, after receiving prophetic seriousness, could jettison the prophetic element and continue freestanding. That is, can rational criticism perdure as a purely secular, critically rational humanism? Tillich unequivocally refutes this pos- sibility. He says, "Through grace even the criticism that has been given prophetic depth is in its turn subjected to criticism. . . . In prophetic criti- cism rational criticism finds both its depth and its limit: its depth through the unconditionedness of the demand, and its limit through grace."[59]

PROPHETIC CRITICISM GIVES DEPTH & SETS LIMITS TO RATIONAL CRITICISM

Prophetic Criticism and Grace

The limiting capacity that prophetic criticism provides for rational criti- cism leads Tillich to refer to prophetic criticism as "the herald of grace."

3 elements of criticism

What remains ambiguous in Tillich's telling is whether prophetic criticism also reaches a limit in grace. Tillich does not claim that limit outright. Does he perhaps imply such a limit when he stresses that rational criticism receives its limit through grace at the point where rational criticism receives prophetic depth? The issue raises the question of how Tillich interprets the relationship between prophetic criticism and grace.

As shown in Luther, Protestant criticism is prophetic criticism

Tillich identifies three necessary elements of criticism—the integrity of both rational and prophetic criticisms, the collaboration of both criticisms, and the "overcoming" of criticism by grace—and finds them dynamically present in Martin Luther's theology.[60] Therefore, "Protestant criticism is prophetic criticism."[61] And yet, justification by faith alone means that even the integrity of a "resistant" existence, based in rational and prophetic criticism against false givenness, does not become the ultimate truth. Tillich makes this statement, we must remember, in the social and political context of Germany in the late 1920s, when someone like Tillich might be most tempted to elevate rational and prophetic resistance to the zenith of Christian life. Even such integrity does not stand on its own feet.

Luther's far reaching influence was due to his ties to rtnl criticism

Regarding the collaboration of rational and prophetic criticism, Tillich claims, "There is little doubt that Luther's far-reaching historical influence was at least partly due to the fact that his thought had an integral relationship to all the significant forms of rational criticism of his age." Those zealous after Luther's legacy—the present author included—need not overlook this most crucial insight of Luther. Tillich notes that those affectionately looking after Luther's legacy often have failed to notice Luther's connection to rational criticism and, thereby, have themselves missed the historical opportunities to make a salutary "Lutheran" difference in their public vocations. Tillich points out that such missed opportunities too often were a mark of his day. Sometimes interpreters of Luther who do recognize how Luther employed a collaborative hermeneutic of the two criticisms—Tillich has Karl Holl in mind—fail to make a significant impact in their own situation. This happens because "they apply directly and immediately to the present those forms of rational criticism contained in Luther's prophetic word."[62] They fail to acknowledge the historically conditioned character of the rational criticism that Luther employed, because they overlook Luther's insight regarding the character of rational criticism *as* historically conditioned. Tillich instead proposes that Luther's heirs allow Luther's lively prophetic use of rational criticism to burst anew out of the present, out of the *kairos*. Perhaps Luther zealots—among

character of his criticism was historically conditioned

whom I count myself—might see themselves analogous to modern-day figure skaters who, while demonstrating expertise in compulsory exercises (the history of Luther's own collaborative hermeneutic of criticism), also cultivate competencies in freestyle skating (contemporary collaborative efforts at rational and prophetic criticism). Still, the compulsories cannot be overlooked in an attempt to go straight to freestyle. Many slip in this way as well and move toward a hermeneutical spirit not traceable to Luther's revolutionary reformation. *CRITICISM MUST BE overcome*

The third element that Tillich finds in Luther's hermeneutic of criticism *BY* is the insight that "criticism be overcome by grace."[63] Tillich designates this *GRACE* element as decisive. Medieval Catholicism had made a fatal mistake, mak- *MEDIEVAL CATH.* ing rational criticism—always connected to moral-ethical criteria—a part *moral y* of grace. Two devastating consequences follow. First, the "unconditioned *make* seriousness of criticism [is] weakened." Second, and increasingly ruinous, *real* the "unconditioned conquest" of critical seriousness dissipates. For Luther *criticsm* and the early reformers, grace symbolized "the situation in which prophetic *A part* criticism is both fulfilled and overcome."[64] Tillich agrees. Here is the answer *of grace* to our question regarding Tillich's understanding of the hermeneutical rela- tionship between prophetic criticism and grace. Because prophetic criti- cism is the herald of grace, grace fulfills the mission of prophetic criticism. Tillich is decisive and clear about this point. Likewise, he is decisive regard- ing grace's "unconditioned conquest" of prophetic criticism.

Why be so decisive about this conquest? What is it about prophetic crit- icism that makes it necessary for it to be "overcome"?[65] Conversely, what is it about grace that would lead someone to question the sole sufficiency of prophetic criticism? What is it about grace that allows it to overcome criti- cism? From the Reformation on, notes Tillich, "the burden of Protes- tantism" has been anchored in its hermeneutic of prophetic criticism. Nevertheless, "Protestantism does not lack the creative and formative prin- ciple; it cannot lack this principle any more than can any other reality. For form is the *prius* of crisis."[66]

The Form of Grace and Religious Culture

Tillich, as he pursues the relationship between prophetic criticism and grace, shows the path he will follow in the second part of his essay. "Ratio- nal form is the presupposition of rational criticism; the form of grace is the presupposition of prophetic criticism."[67] His thesis is that "prophetic criti- cism is itself supported by some being, by some religious form from which

[Handwritten margin note: PROPHETIC CRITICISM SPEAKS IN THE NAME OF IN A TRANSCENDENT BEING THAT ALSO BELONGS TO REALITY]

criticism proceeds."[68] He quickly notes that this "being" "cannot be concretely grasped" as one can examine and come to understand something finite like an animal or a tree or even another human person." He is reflecting on the relationship between transcendence and immanence, on the relationship between "beyond" reality and "belonging" to reality. "If prophetic criticism speaks in the name of any being at all, this being must be transcendent being, which, despite its transcendent character, must also belong to reality." "Grace . . . [is] transcendent reality as something present," and, therefore, "[p]rophetic criticism must burst forth from the reality of grace or—to keep the analogy—it must issue from a form of grace."[69] This involves the problem of "religious form-creation."

[Handwritten margin note: FOR TILLICH THIS IS GRACE, IT GIVES RISE TO THE PROB of RELIGIOUS FORM CREATION]

Tillich investigates religious form-creation by steering clear of two false interpretations. The first false interpretation begins by viewing the relational bond between prophetic and rational criticism as one of identity. This interpretation would mean that grace appears in rational criticism that had reached perfection, surrendering the inevitability and seriousness of prophetic criticism and reducing grace to rational forms and, thus, effectively dissolving grace. The second false interpretation begins by taking grace as "something objective because it is present."[70] In this false interpretation, grace becomes "fixed and tangible in the same way as any other reality," and thereby identifiable with a particular institution "exempt from criticism." In both false interpretations the character of grace itself "is destroyed because of preoccupation with the form."

[Handwritten margin note: GRACE ISN'T IN RTN CRITICISM OR A FIXED INSTITUTION (CHURCH)]

In the face of these powerfully destructive false interpretations, why not "give up the whole conception, form of grace"?[71] That, argues Tillich, represents the path taken by Barth's dialectical theology. Still, even dialectical theology is "compelled to indicate the being from whom its prophetic criticism proceeds." The concept of the form of grace remains "unavoidable, for it is the presupposition of any criticism uttered with ultimate power and authority."

[Handwritten margin note: BUT NOT SIMPLY WEI AS BARTH DID, GIVE UP THE WHOLE CONCEPT OR FORM OF GRACE]

"Grace," claims Tillich, "is something present but not something objective. It is actual in objects, not as an object but as the transcendent meaning of an object. The form of grace is a form of [transcendent] meaning. . . . Thus reality can become the bearer of a meaning that unconditionally transcends it. And wherever this meaning exists, we have a form or *Gestalt* of grace."[72] "Form of grace" can be perceived, but not as an object alongside other objects. It can be, as Tillich states three times within a single paragraph, "intuitively perceived."

[Handwritten margin note: FORM OF GRACE ISN'T IN AN OBJECT, BUT IN TRANSCENDENT MEANING OF THE OBJECT. IT CAN BE INTUITIVELY PERCEIVED.]

Form of grace is an anticipation of what is beyond both freedom or being. It is an eschatological anticipation.

Tillich turns to "eschatological thinking" to explain the relationship *that* between the perceptibility and the nonobjective character of "form of *can it* grace."[73] "Anticipation" is the key. "Inherent in anticipation is a temporal *Be possessed,* image of a perfect consummation that is coming. This temporal image is a *it* symbolic form essential to all eschatological thinking; it cannot be dis- *can* pensed with, although its directness can be broken. But if it is used—even *one* as something 'broken'—then the form of grace may be characterized as an *Be a* anticipation of what is beyond both freedom and being." Still, warns *figurative laying* Tillich, anticipatory modes of participation in "form of grace" should never *hold* be received as a possession at one's disposal.[74] Such possessing violates the *of* structure of eschatological anticipation, in which "the thing anticipated *something* *cannot yet* be appropriated." Anticipation "is as it were a figurative laying *that* *is* hold of something that is imbued with meaning, but which must not be *imbued w/* objectified." *meaning*

As the third step in exploring Protestantism as a creative and formative principle, Tillich attends to the relationship between rational forms and *rtnl* "form of grace," a relationship that parallels that between rational criticism *forms* *receiv* and prophetic criticism. "[T]he form of grace is realized only in rational *a new* forms and in such a way that, on the one hand, it [the form of grace] gives *dimension* to them a meaning that transcends them, while on the other hand, it unites *of* with the particular meaning inherent in rational forms."[75] That is, rational *transcendent* forms receive a *new dimension* of transcendent meaning, and the form of *meaning* grace, which includes rational forms within itself, acquires its "different expressions."[76] *Expressions of the form of grace.*

Tillich designates these different expressions of the form of grace "reli- *are* gious culture."[77] As he explores the mission of criticism in regard to reli- *part* gious culture, he saturates his inquiry with special urgency. Religious *of* culture as an expression of the form of grace is *"religious culture"*

> subject to criticism, to rational as well as to prophetic criticism.
> Indeed, they [religious cultural expressions] are the special object
> of prophetic criticism. For it is the continual task of prophetic crit-
> icism to fight against the confusion of the "form of grace" with
> "religious culture." It is the objectification of the form of grace
> that leads to confusion. Here, it is manifest in man's [*sic*] attempt
> to exploit grace in order to escape criticism.[78]

Tillich's experience of the triumphalistic and pretentious *Kulturprotes-
tantismus*—cultural Protestantism—of nineteenth-century German Protes-

tant liberalism, which permeated Germany as it entered World War I, leads him to espouse special alertness to the idolatrous "danger that these forms of expression may claim to be the immediate expression of the form of grace." Such watchfulness remains the core of the Christian prophetic imagination.

Even so, the eradication or even emaciation of religious culture would also be disastrous. A ditch of secularism would open up on the other side. True, "the holy can appear in the garment of secularism."[79] And true, the secular appearance of the holy "represents by its mere existence a criticism" of the absolute objectification of any religious culture or religious form of grace, and this "proves that grace can operate independently of religious culture."[80] Still, priority cannot remain with secular culture, "for it too is in danger of denying the form of grace in favor of a mere self-enclosed form of being, and of becoming autonomous, cutting itself off from any transcendent meaning." To avoid this ditch, Tillich investigates the integration of religious culture, rational form, and the transcendence of the form of grace.

> Religious culture is the epitome of all those forms in which the rational form expresses its transcendent meaning and in which the rational form receives by anticipation the character of a form of grace. The existential forms of all churches and all individual piety have this meaning. They are nothing in themselves. In themselves, they are merely rational forms; but they express a transcendent meaning that can appear in the rational form.[81]

The possibility of this integration leads us to investigate the communicative turn within critical social theory and the contribution that this turn can make toward prophetic reasoning and the Christian imagination.

The Form of Grace and the Protestant Congregation

Tillich perceives that Barth's theological supernaturalism, which tends toward prophetic suppression of the very notion of the form of grace, unwittingly and ironically promotes autonomous secularism. In this ironic way, Barthian supernaturalism becomes the flip side of versions of rational criticism that ideologically and positivistically reject prophetic depth. Autonomous secularism intentionally practices "a missing" of grace; supernaturalism unknowingly practices a "squandering of grace."[82] Without rootedness in the form of grace an autonomous, secularist culture lacks "the power to be, that is, the power to participate in unconditioned or transcendent being." By ignoring the form of grace anticipated in religious culture, autonomous secularity eventually becomes "absolutely impotent." This parallels the warning that Tillich extended to Marcuse, of criticism becoming "positivistic and contingent." If autonomous secularity rejects religious culture, why does it not become impotent immediately? Unwittingly, argues Tillich, autonomous secularity "lives on the inheritance of the form of grace out of which it was born, namely, the Protestant Christian tradition."

Tillich acknowledges that surprise often erupts at the suggestion that Protestantism could embody a form of grace. Surprise arises for two historically situated reasons. First, Protestantism emerged in Western Christianity as a prophetic protest against Roman Catholic objectifications of the form of grace. This prophetic protest emerges as a basic Protestant characteristic. Second, Protestantism continued as a dynamic reality because it redirected its prophetic protest away from Roman Catholicism and toward autonomous secularization. Still, argues Tillich, Protestantism must be more than critical protest, because grace always "is the *prius* of criticism."[83] For this reason, Tillich aims for a "positive approach" to Protestantism's formative powers.

Traditionally, claims Tillich, Protestantism preserved one form of grace after shattering Roman Catholicism's objectified forms, namely, Scripture. That form has since broken down, because Protestant orthodoxy reduced Scripture to fixed and imperviously dogmatic formulations. This has brought Protestantism to "the verge of collapse."[84] A second attempt at a Protestant expression of the form of grace came as Protestantism found a connecting point with Catholicism "by laicizing the monastic ideal of interior discipline."[85] Tillich argues that this venture did not endure because, in Protestantism, a person "is holy not because he symbolized a form of grace [as with the Catholic saint] but, rather, because he has received the forgiveness of sins. He is holy in his unholiness. Here the application of the concept of holiness necessarily involves a paradox, and hence it can never result in a form or *Gestalt*."[86]

As Tillich sees it, the paradoxical unworkableness of laicizing monastic interior discipline did, in fact, engender a new form of grace of "immeasurable historical significance, namely, the heroic personality."[87] "The heroic personality is aware of the boundary situation of man and always subjects himself to prophetic as well as to ethical rational criticism. His seriousness, his dignity, his great majesty—to use a term often applied to Calvin—is based on the fact that he refuses to allow the depths of prophetic criticism to be covered over and hidden by any objective form of grace." The greatness of this prophetically self-critical, heroic personality "is at the same time its danger." Because this heroic Protestant has no recourse to a Protestant expression of the form of grace, it is "almost inevitable" that the heroic personality will take on the rational form of ethical personality. Embodied only in this form, the heroic personality will accept only rational criticism as it seeks the constant improvement of the humanistic ideal. This process, as Tillich notes, crowds out the unconditionality of prophetic criticism and leads to a pretentious, self-sufficient, autonomous personhood.

Despite the continuous breakup of the heroic personality on the anvil of self-sufficient autonomy, this Protestant course is "always retarded . . . by the fact that within Protestantism the *Gestalt* of grace has never disappeared completely."[88] This is true because "the form of grace is precisely the presupposition of prophetic criticism," and, therefore, it could never be absent where prophetic criticism is effective. Tillich continues: "The Protestant is holy because of the judgment [of unholiness] that is pronounced upon him, but this is true only if he applies this judgment to himself, that is, only if he has faith. But faith is possible only by virtue of the Holy Spirit, that is, in a form of grace." Protestantism's formative and creative power, Tillich says, is frequently underrated but still has become a historical reality primarily in shaping the personal life.[89] This happened with intensity in Protestant pietism. Tillich thinks that, in this way, even the bourgeois personality and the romantic personality retain some facet—though highly secularized—of the formative power of Protestantism.

There remains yet one more line of inquiry that Tillich pursues regarding a Protestant form of grace. This Protestant form is the congregation. Tillich judges this Protestant expression less significant than shaping the personal life, because the congregation resides, as he says, "in the specifically religious sphere."[90] He apparently means that this Protestantly embodied form of grace has not had a broad-based consequence in culture or civilization.[91] He quickly adds, however, that Protestantism did not create the congregation but selected from the many available Catholic forms.

Tillich interprets the congregation as that "which is supposed to pass on to the individual the 'pure doctrine' found in Scripture."[92] In this light, its "proper function . . . is to provide the sermon and the catechetical, liturgical preparation and guidance for understanding the sermon." He continues, "But the congregation is rarely if ever thought of as a visible form of grace. Hence, Protestantism is deprived of any real power in the religious sphere of creative cultural activity. . . . From this point of view the decline in its [Protestantism's] power of attraction is quite understandable." With this lament he seems to accept as inevitable his definition of the congregation, and his description tends to remain that of a heteronomous institution. Does he think that the Protestant congregation continued as it had existed within Catholicism, from which Protestantism had borrowed it? But was the Protestant congregation left unreformed, at least in the formative years of the Reformation?

Did Tillich harbor hope in 1929 that the congregation could be reconstituted in the direction of a theonomous institution? I cannot say for sure. As he ponders whether Protestantism can become a form of grace in reality, Tillich mulls over three things, the first of which touches on the notion of a congregation. First, the congregation would have to consider itself "an explicit expression of the transcendent significance of all sociological forms."[93] Two misperceptions would have to be avoided. On the one hand, the congregation could not regard itself as above other forms of social life. Rather, congregations would purport to be "only the bearers of the transcendent significance" of secular forms of existence. On the other hand, the congregation could not exist in such a way that it would dissolve into another secular structure. Rather, "[w]hat is required is the sort of church in which the social forms may contemplate the representation of their own transcendent import of meaning and the anticipation of their own ultimate goal beyond being and freedom." What is Tillich inferring? It seems that he is imagining a reflexive form of congregation in close companionship with other social institutions and in service of these other institutions' reflexivity. We will keep this in mind in exploring the communicative turn in critical social theory and in considering congregations as communicatively prophetic public companions.

Tillich identifies *history* as a second route for refashioning Protestant expressions of the form of grace. On the one hand, he strives to avoid a rigid Protestant objectification. On the other hand, he wants to avoid the church-above-history tendency that accompanied Roman Catholicism. "History is the *locus* of the essences. The idea exists within history, not beyond it. The form of grace always strives for realization in the changing historical forms."[94] Tillich inserts his famous notion of *kairos,* that is, "fulfilled time, . . . the realization of the form of grace in a new entity."[95]

Tillich offers a third and final factor for refashioning Protestant expressions of the form of grace. "When the idea of a form of grace is adopted by Protestantism and somehow brought to reality, then Protestant personalism is by that very fact overcome; and this holds for the psychological as well as the social aspect of Protestant personalism."[96] By "Protestant personalism" Tillich means the kind of heroic figure often found in Protestant pietism. This heroic individual or group stands alone on the rock of autonomous choice, self-defining, self-sustaining, self-sufficient. Such heroic figures remain isolated, supposing they are not indebted to the wisdom of previous generations or heritages. Such decisionistic personalism would cease with a different Protestant expression of the form of grace. For prior to any moment or act of decision there exists "the anticipation of the eschaton in the existential order." This eschatological anticipation does not obliterate the psychic and social character of personality, but provides the encompassing condition that makes personal decision possible. In 1929, Tillich thinks that "religious socialism" might manifest this eschatological anticipation existentially, although he quickly admits that the outcome "cannot be predicted in our present situation." How right he was.

Unfortunately, Tillich does not reflect, within the context of the Protestant congregation, either on the notion of history or on anticipation of the eschaton in the existential order. How might we inquire with more historical and eschatological depth into the character of reflexive ecclesial communities? This would help us address more fully Tillich's most significant question: "Can Protestantism become in reality a form of grace and at the same time maintain its unswerving pursuit of prophetic criticism, a criticism that it cannot weaken without destroying its own character?"[97] We return to some of these issues in chapter 6, in which we consider the renewal of Christian prophetic imagination. Dennis McCann's discussion of Tillich's religious socialism offers an important insight as we proceed.

The Critique of Oracular Prophetism

McCann investigates Tillich's religious socialism as a possible model for contemporary theology and does so in the context of Juan Luis Segundo's liberation theology and Reinhold Niebuhr's Christian realism.[98] Within McCann's largely appreciative account of Tillich's coming to a "socialist decision," we briefly engage one of McCann's two chief criticisms. McCann focuses on Tillich's notion of *kairos* in relationship to Christian prophetism. For Tillich, the dilemma of Christian prophetism is to respond to the *kairos* without straying either into excessive supernaturalistic spiritualism (as happened with Barth) or reductionistic, politicized, cultural secularism (as happened with nineteenth-century liberal Protestantism). According to McCann, Tillich's conceptualization of *kairos* appears too intuitionistic and too oracular.

> The problem here is what, after all, is the basis for the decision that Tillich demands we make? From whatever angle I approach it, the answer always depends on Tillich's sense of the *Kairos*. In light of the *Kairos,* religious socialism discovers the form of grace in the proletarian situation. But what is the *Kairos* but Tillich's own deeply personal discernment of history's meaning? Moreover, can Tillich's personal authority provide a sufficient warrant for making "the socialist decision"? The difficulty for me becomes even more pressing when I consider the subsequent fluctuation in Tillich's sense of the *Kairos.* Since his theology reflects "a deepening 'sacred void' of waiting" in the years after World War II, apparently I am asked to accept this passing of the *Kairos* once again on the strength of Tillich's personal authority. What I find distressing about his pronouncements on the *Kairos* over the years is their oracular quality. I am stymied, in short, not because I assume that existential decisions should be so tightly argued as to be virtually risk-free; but because Tillich's use of the *Kairos* principle remains just too intuitive to provide much help in checking the reasonableness of "the unconditional demand" mediated through it.[99]

For McCann, Tillich's intuitionism remains too decisionistic, expressivistic, and mystical.[100] Further, Tillich's intuitionism seems sundered from reasonableness and thus from checking—from the testing of others.[101] Tillich's intuitionism seems to lead inevitably toward the *oracular.* Though McCann does not make this statement, perhaps we would not be far from the mark to observe how fully Tillich and his audience imbibe in the heroic personalism that Tillich found problematic, as seen above.

Is "oracular" the inevitable epithet for the Christian prophetic imagination? Must we summon the courage to be "oracular," "sin boldly" in an oracular sense, or be oracularly "faithful" rather than effective? As we inquire into the Christian prophetic imagination, perhaps we might reframe McCann's intuitionistic, oracular critique of Tillich in this way: how might we construe a nonoracular, Christian prophetic imagination? Without abandoning the collaborative dynamics that exist in Protestantism as a critical and creative principle, which Tillich has identified, what other elements are needed to develop a Christian prophetic imagination? In the final footnote of McCann's appreciative critique, he hints that one would need "something similar" to Habermas's theory of public discourse.[102]

We now turn to Habermas's work and focus on three facets of his thought as he retrieves and refashions critical theory. With the term *critical,* we revisit the relationship of criticism and normative criteria and how that relationship becomes a point of contention between Habermas and Horkheimer/Adorno. With the term *theory,* we investigate the theory of communicative reason and action. This communicative turn in critical social theory can help the prophetic imagination overcome the intuitionistic, decisionistic, and oracular temptations. With the term *social,* we investigate Habermas's historical and conceptual account of the new "civil society" emerging in the West, and its import for development of "deliberative democracy." This investigation will help situate the Christian prophetic imagination in a nonoracular space, or, rather, to refashion oracular and hierarchical social spaces into more participatory and deliberative spaces.

PART TWO

Enter Habermas—
The Communicative
Imagination

3

Criticism:
The Transformation of Critique

In chapter 2 we noted Tillich's deep concern that critique would burn itself out were it not anchored in the ultimate. A similar concern emerges in the work of Jürgen Habermas. During the 1960s, Habermas presented himself as a defender of the heritage of the Frankfurt School of critical social theory. His defense took shape as he sided with Theodor Adorno against the proponents of rational positivism. In the social sciences and in philosophy, this debate is known as "the positivist dispute."[1] Habermas sides with Adorno in this dispute, despite the fact that he differs with how Horkheimer and Adorno developed critical social theory during the 1940s. He remains in continuity with the basic intention of critical social theory as it originated in the 1930s. He opposes the new direction introduced by Horkheimer and Adorno during the 1940s, because it "consumes the critical impulse itself."[2] His appraisal resembles Tillich's criticism of Marcuse a generation earlier, except Tillich's critique, unlike Habermas's, was assertively "theological."

In this chapter, I outline Habermas's portrayal of Horkheimer and Adorno's path during the 1940s. This will prepare us to consider in chapter 4 Habermas's reasons for a *change of paradigm* in critical social theory.[3] First, I recall one of Horkheimer's core convictions during the 1930s, which he shared with Marx, distinguishing between traditional theory and critical social theory. I point out the situations in the late 1930s and early 1940s that led Horkheimer to abandon this conviction and thus the original conceptualization of critical social theory. Second, I investigate Horkheimer's search for a new conceptual basis for critical social theory. Briefly stated, Horkheimer borrows an insight from Max Weber's diagnosis of the modern Western situation and couples this Weberian insight with an insight borrowed from Georg Lukács's analysis of capitalism. By combining the Weberian and Lukácsian insights, Horkheimer reconceptualizes critical social theory as a "critique of instrumental rationality." Third, I examine Habermas's appraisal of Horkheimer and Adorno's critique of instrumental rationality and why it eventually "consumes the critical impulse itself." Habermas argues, instead, for a transformation of critique that can energize critical social theory and, indeed, criticism itself.

Abandoning a Core Conviction

Habermas points to the preface to *Dialectic of Enlightenment,* in which Horkheimer and Adorno admit that they "were forced to abandon" the most basic conviction that had undergirded Horkheimer's conceptualization of critical social theory during the 1930s, a conviction they shared with Marx.[4] What was this conviction? Horkheimer believed that a rational potential resides within Western capitalist society. This latent though powerful seed of reason exists in the great bourgeois ideals of freedom, justice, brotherhood. These great ideals only exist, however, as the potentiality for a rational society, but not as Western society's fully functioning rationale. The overwhelming poverty and immense suffering of the proletariat within capitalist society provided the evidence for Horkheimer that, as of yet, these ideals exist merely as rational potentiality. Still, his conviction included the hope that the rational potential of these normative ideals could be tapped and unleashed to critique the ideology of capitalism.

Proceeding from this conviction, Horkheimer based his 1930s-styled critical theory of society on the notion of an "immanent critique." That is, normative rational ideals, which function as standards for critically evaluating Western capitalist society as well as for redesigning and rebuilding a different society, are themselves present ("immanent") within the capitalist social system itself. Immanent critique summons "the existent [society], in its historical context, with the claim of its conceptual principles, in order to criticize the relation between the two and thus transcend them."[5] As seen in chapter 1, one of the crucial conceptual nuts to crack during the 1930s was "who" would be the agent(s) to tap into this rational potential and "how" this agent would do it. These questions appear at the points where theory and practice connect. Early in the 1930s, Horkheimer, in agreement with Marx, thought that the proletariat itself—the industrial working class— would be the agent.[6] Because of its economic location, the proletariat would come to a consciousness of Western society's rational potential and would, as the critical prophetic class, protest the capitalist social system on the basis of these rational ideals. Finally, the proletariat would actualize these ideals in rebuilding the West as a new socialist society. By the time of the 1937 programmatic essay "Traditional and Critical Theory," Horkheimer had started looking for a new agent to take up the immanent critique of capitalist ideology. The new prophetic agents appeared to be the critical theorists themselves! These aloof intellectuals, surmised Horkheimer, possessed prophetic awareness of the contradictions of capitalism as well as philosophical insight into the rational potential inherent in Western ideals.

This 1937 exchange of agents introduced new dilemmas into critical social theory. Because of their social location in the academy, critical theorists lacked meaningful connections to existing political organizations that could bring about the rebuilding of a new rational society. This situation raised the question about a split between theory and real political praxis. By viewing their own theory work itself as a form of praxis, these critical theorists mitigated the problem somewhat. Still, their theorizing remained too disconnected from possible agents to incarnate their theoretical work, bringing a new fissure between theory and praxis.

The 1937 change of agents also introduced a second dilemma. Horkheimer eventually realized that he no longer was an ordinary Marxist, an orthodox Marxist. Still, in his self-understanding, he had not become non-Marxist. First, like Marx, he still was deeply troubled by the poverty and suffering of the working class. Second, like Marx, he still thought that the capitalist mode of production was the prime culprit for this suffering. Third, like Marx, he held to the conviction regarding immanent critique. He knew, however, that when he dispensed with the proletariat as the revolutionary agent and searched for a new agent, he had introduced a major wrinkle into Marxism. As a social philosophy, Marxist theory itself existed as a social and historical product and could not be hypostatized and dogmatized. Marxism ought not become a rigid orthodoxy, cryogenically preserved, waiting to be released at a technologically enhanced time and place. Because Marxist theory itself remained closely tied to ongoing social and historical processes, Horkheimer's critical theory could be expected to change and develop as the sociohistorical situation changed. What historical developments led Horkheimer both toward a nondogmatic, nonorthodox type of Marxism and toward the search for a new prophetic-revolutionary agent?

Two historical situations emerged during the 1930s that, taken together, contributed to Horkheimer's deserting hope that the proletariat would be the revolutionary agent. First, fascism in Western Europe developed a race-based kind of monopoly capitalism that deftly—and demonically—absorbed the revolutionary potential of organized labor and co-opted it for its racist ideology. This devastated Horkheimer. Second, Soviet-style Marxism moved toward accelerated bureaucratization. Eventually this trend devolved into Stalin's bloody form of coercive socialist organization and the Soviet Communist Party. These two developments sent Horkheimer searching. Still, in 1937 he retained the fundamental conviction that true reason was immanent within the ideals of Western society. The rationality of Western ideals as the basis of immanent critique warranted the search for a new prophetic-emancipatory agent. This conviction would soon change.

When Horkheimer and the other institute members fled Nazi Germany, they came into contact with other Western capitalist countries. The "New Deal" in the United States demonstrated capitalism's ameliorative side. Capitalism's pacifying capacity could provide a softer landing, a "safety net" for those who inevitably fall through the sharp-edged cracks of capitalism's machinery. But this capacity did not alter the basic machinery of capitalism and did not satisfy Horkheimer. The United States's amelioratory capitalism, taken in combination with the situations in Nazi Germany and Stalinist Soviet Union, led Horkheimer toward a more complete disappointment in his earlier revolutionary expectations.

At the beginning of the 1940s, Horkheimer comes to a new and radicalized realization. Not only must he abandon hope that the proletariat would be the agent of the prophetic critique and reconstruction of Western society, but he also must discard the most basic conviction of his critical social theory until that time. He was no longer convinced that an immanent rationality existed in Western society that could serve as the normative standard for critique and reconstruction. This shift also implied, though Horkheimer did not admit it during the 1940s, that he would have to abandon his interdisciplinary, social science research projects. For the very idea of social research projects presupposed that the social sciences were, in fact, harbingers of the vestiges of reason. The historical disappointments led to theoretical disillusionment in the potential of reason itself and, thus, in the potential for a rational society, for a just society.

Horkheimer's changed mood and conceptual orientation shows in his 1946 preface to his 1944 lectures, published under the title *Eclipse of Reason:*

At the moment of this writing, the peoples of the democratic nations are comforted with the problems of consummating their victory of arms. They must work out and put into practice the principles of humanity in the name of which the sacrifices of war were made. The present potentialities of social achievement surpass the expectations of all the philosophers and statesmen who have ever outlined in utopian programs the idea of a truly human society. Yet there is a universal feeling of fear and disillusionment. The hopes of mankind seem to be farther from fulfillment today than they were even in the groping epochs when they were first formulated by humanists.[7]

In the face of this disillusionment, Horkheimer completely reconsiders and reconceptualizes *reason:*

It seems that even as technical knowledge expands the horizon of man's thoughts and activity, his autonomy as an individual, his ability to resist the growing apparatus of mass manipulation, his power of imagination, his independent judgment appear to be reduced. Advance in technical facilities for enlightenment is accompanied by a process of dehumanization. Thus progress threatens to nullify the very goal it is supposed to realize—the idea of man. . . . As understood and practiced in our civilization, progressive rationalization tends, in my opinion, to obliterate that very substance of reason in the name of which this progress is espoused.[8]

The Critique of Instrumental Reason

When Horkheimer jettisons the conviction that a rational standard for a just society is immanent within Western society, he does not forsake the certainty that Western society is rational. On the contrary, more than ever he knows Western society to be eminently enlightened, rigorously rational, and, indeed, progressively so. What changes is his opinion of what Western reason—Enlightenment rationality—is, or, at least, has become. By the early 1940s, Horkheimer has become self-conscious of having changed his entire orientation toward reason. This change surfaces in two books, *Dialectic of Enlightenment,* coauthored with Theodor Adorno, and *Eclipse of Reason,* Horkheimer's lectures from 1944.

Max Weber's Influence

We can observe the sea change in Horkheimer's thinking about reason if we place his thoughts into a grid comparing strong versus weak, good versus bad. Before 1940, he considered reason to be "good" in the sense of "a good" to be sought after, a goal worthy of pursuit, a moral potentiality that ought to be actualized. But, because morally "good reason" dwelt in a "bad" capitalist society, it existed in an unrealized condition. Therefore, Horkheimer deemed "good reason" to be politically "weak." Still, "weak reason" has the potential to become politically "strong." The theorist's task was, on the one hand, to discover, analyze, and promulgate "morally good but politically weak" reason and, on the other hand, to identify and encourage a prophetic ("good") and revolutionary ("strong") agent who would convert "good but weak" reason into "morally good and politically strong" reason.

After 1940, Horkheimer considered Western reason since the time of the eighteenth-century Enlightenment already to have been politically "strong" and becoming stronger. But he also considered "politically strong-and-becoming-stronger" reason to be "bad" reason rather than good reason. His paradigm shifts from the pre-1940 concept of a "good-but-weak-with-the-potential-for-getting-stronger" reason to the post-1940 concept of a "strong-and-getting-stronger-but-bad-and-becoming-evermore-evil" reason. This paradigm shift comes about as he adopts Max Weber's analysis of the Western "type" of reason.[9]

Weber proposed a conceptual distinction between two types of reason—formal and substantive—embodied in Western society.[10] Further, within formal rationality Weber distinguished between "instrumental rationality" and "rationality of choice."[11] Generally speaking, Weber characterized formal rationality as *Zweckrationalität,* that is, as "purposive rationality." Purposive rationality was Weber's core concept for explaining the Western process of modernization.

Horkheimer admits that Weber's distinction between purposive rationality and substantive rationality "resembles to a certain degree" his own distinction between subjective reason and objective reason.[12] By the early 1940s, Horkheimer recognizes that he had based his earlier conviction about the potential for reason on the unexamined assumption that Western reason simply meant objective-substantial rationality. By objective or substantial rationality Horkheimer means the rationale of social ideals like justice. The distinction between subjective and objective reason, which he makes in the early 1940s, helps him to realize that the substantialist or objective type of rationality had permeated the classical philosophies of Plato and Aristotle, of medieval scholasticism and German Idealism. Despite the variety of these philosophical orientations, they all postulated and then sought to examine an objective or real order of substantial normative reasonableness. These philosophical systems recognized the existence of an order or hierarchy, a totality, an inclusive human reality. This objective totality functioned like a natural template, providing the moral rationale for the patterns of social life. In these formulations of objective reason, the emphasis was always "on ends rather than means."[13] Accordingly, objective, substantial reality anchored the great Western ideals. According to these comprehensive philosophical systems, the "degree of reasonableness of a man's life could be determined according to its harmony with this totality . . . [with] the objective order of the 'reasonable.'"[14]

In the classic philosophical traditions of the West, someone could appraise the thinking, acting, and living of any subject, whether the subject were an individual or a group or a society or even a civilization, on the basis of the degree of reasonable harmony with the total order. Horkheimer refers to this reasonable harmony as "subjective reason." He notes that, in the classic philosophical traditions, research into the makeup of subjective reason most often took a back seat to detailed analyses of the structure of objective reason. Subjective rationality depended, therefore, on the degree of conformity that subjective reason displayed in relation to the objective order of the reasonable. The great traditions could even assess self-interest and self-preservation, whether of an individual or a civilization, to be "rational" to the degree that self-interest or self-preservation fit harmoniously within the totality of reality. Horkheimer's pre-1940 conviction that the objective order of the reasonable embodied itself to one degree or another in the subjective reason of persons, groups, societies, or a civilization appeared erroneous in his post-1940 analyses.

After 1940, Horkheimer would no longer see Western, enlightened rationality as the progressive unleashing into subjective reason of the potential of objective, substantial reasonableness, which the classic philosophies had theorized. Rather, and in basic agreement with Weber, Horkheimer felt that the eighteenth-century Enlightenment had unleashed a different type of reason altogether. Weber called it "purposive rationality," Horkheimer calls it "instrumental reason." Furthermore, this instrumental type of reasoning "underlies our contemporary industrial culture" and does so in a radical, total, and destructive way.[15]

From 1940 on, Horkheimer executes a thoroughgoing "critique of instrumental reason."[16] This critique rests on a typological distinction between objective-substantial reason, on the one hand, and instrumental reason, on the other. He underscores the historical significance that this distinction makes by recounting (1) the historical circumstances through which instrumental reason emerged; (2) how instrumental reason became the dominant and eventually the exclusive form of Western reason; and (3) the consequences brought about by this "transformation of reason into a mere instrument."[17]

The Emergence of Instrumental Reason

Horkheimer, like many others, points out that modern Western rationalism gained a foothold during the aftermath of the devastating religious wars of the latter part of the sixteenth century and the first half of the seventeenth century. The Peace of Westphalia in 1648 ended the Thirty Years' War, in which Catholics, Lutherans, and Calvinists slaughtered each other along confessional lines. Philosophical rationalism promoted itself as a more effective social glue, as a more reliable basis for social peace and economic prosperity than the divided Christian religion could provide.

> [W]hen [seventeenth-century rationalist] philosophy began to supplant religion, it did not intend to abolish objective truth, but was attempting only to give it a new rational foundation. The contention in regard to the nature of the absolute was not the main ground on which [the rational] metaphysicians were persecuted and tortured [by the Christian hierarchies]. The real issue was whether revelation or reason, whether theology or philosophy, should be the agency for determining and expressing ultimate truth.[18]

Nevertheless, stresses Horkheimer, both Christianity and rationalist philosophy maintained "complete agreement" that a real totality existed. They disagreed only on how to access that totality, whether by means of the church's authoritarian interpretation of revelation or by philosophical reason and analysis.

The controversy ended in a stalemate. Reason would rule the public realms of politics and society, and revelation would rule the private and ecclesiastical realms. Horkheimer points out the devastating consequences that this compartmentalized stalemate would have for both religion and reason.

People have gradually become reconciled to the idea that each [religion and philosophical rationalism] lives its own life within the walls of its cultural compartment, tolerating the other. The neutralization of religion, now reduced to the status of one cultural good among others, contradicted its "total" claim that it incorporates objective truth, and also emasculated it. Although religion remained respected on the surface, its neutralization paved the way for its elimination as the medium of spirited objectivity, itself.patterned after the idea of the absoluteness of religious revelation.

In reality the contexts of both philosophy and religion have been deeply affected by this peaceful settlement of their original content. The philosophers of the Enlightenment attacked religion in the name of reason; in the end what they killed was not the church but metaphysics and the objective concept of reason itself, the source of power of their own efforts. . . . Reason has liquidated itself as an agency of ethical, moral, and religious insight. . . .

Religion seemingly profited from this development. . . . At the same time, however, its neutrality means the wasting away of its real spirit, its relatedness to truth, once believed to be the same in science, art, and politics, and for all mankind. The death of speculative [reflective] religion, at first religion's servant and later its foe, may prove catastrophic for religion itself.[19]

The Nature and Effect of Instrumental Reason

The rapid emergence in the West of instrumental reason obliterated the traditions of objective-substantial rationality. Unlike the objective-substantial type of reason, instrumental reason does not focus on the rationale of various ends or of the template, order, or hierarchy of the totality of reality. On the contrary, with instrumental reason "[t]here is no reasonable aim as such, and to discuss the superiority of one aim over another in terms of reason becomes meaningless."[20] Where instrumental reason reigns,

> thinking cannot be of any help in determining the desirability of any goal in itself. The acceptability of ideals, the criteria for our actions and beliefs, the leading principles of ethics and politics, all our ultimate decisions are made to depend upon factors other than reason. They are supposed to be matters of [private and personal] choice and predilection, and [under the reign of instrumental reason] it has become meaningless to speak of truth in making practical, moral, or esthetic decisions.[21]

Instrumental reason deals only with means, not ends. It consists of "the ability to calculate probabilities and thereby to co-ordinate the right means" to achieve any end or purpose. The rationality of instrumental reason refers only to the efficiency and effectiveness of a selected means—the goal is not important. "Since ends are no longer determined in the light of reason, it is impossible to say that one economic or political system, no matter how cruel and despotic, is less reasonable than any other." Instrumental rationality "serves any particular endeavor, good or bad. It is a tool of all action of society, but it must not try to set the patterns of social and individual life, which are assumed to be set by other forces." The rationality of instrumental reason only exists as "the classification of facts and the calculation of probabilities. . . . Reason has become an instrument."[22]

Weber's influence appears not only in Horkheimer's critique of instrumental reason, but also in his diagnosis of the consequences of instrumental reason's progressive dominance over Western society and its ways of living. Weber argued that the rise of purposive rationality led to the disenchantment of the world and of religious worldviews. Further, this disenchantment led Western people progressively to experience a loss of meaning, which historically had been provided by the integrating power either of a religiously revealed or rationally accessed totality. Under the reign of instrumental reason, "[m]eaning is supplanted by function or effect in the world of things and events."[23] Whatever meaning remains in life becomes tethered to self-preservation and thus to self-interest.[24]

In a society in bondage to instrumental reason, a loss of freedom accompanies the loss of meaning. According to Weber's analysis, purposive rationality finds its most potent application in the rational functioning of social organizations. Weber famously states that progressive rational bureaucratization of society, particularly in the economy and the state, forces society into an "iron cage."[25] Horkheimer argues that the increase in instrumental rationality ushers in a "change in the character of freedom."[26] On the one hand, the reign of instrumental reason brings an unprecedented multiplication of material choices—consumer choices—for people to make. On the other hand, along with this sheer multiplicity of choices comes an increasing pressure, even coercion, to make choices, but without the possibility that these choices are rational choices. This is true because reason, having been reduced to a tool of efficiency, no longer entails ends, goals, ideals, or purposes beyond self-preservation and, thus, self-interest. In this way, freedom itself becomes part of self-interest.

The Influence of Georg Lukács

Horkheimer sharpens his own diagnosis of the modern loss of freedom by yoking the features of instrumental reason to Lukács's insights regarding the modern phenomenon of "reification." Lukács tried to uncover the most basic form of existence or way of life that governed modern Western society and, by extension, that governed each individual. He settled on the concept of *reification* as the dominant form of modern social existence in the West. He argues that reification becomes so predominant in modern capitalist society that it determines how individuals interpret everything. Reification determines the interpretation of nature, of interpersonal relations, and even of the subjective natural world of people's own bodies. Reification as a mode of existence regards every relationship as a "thing." Reification means "thingification." "The domination of nature," notes Horkheimer, "involves the domination of man."[27] Every relationship—whether with the natural world or one's own body, whether with friends, neighbors, or community, whether with personal experiences—becomes an "it." Reification converts every human reality into an object to be scanned, surveyed, handled, manipulated, and controlled. Further, under capitalism, the potential of any and every "thing" dwells in its potential as a commodity. Invariably, therefore, reification means commodification.

"Reification is typical" of instrumental rationality, Horkheimer claims.[28] "Reification is a process that can be traced back to the beginnings of organized society and the use of tools. However, the transformation of all products of human activity into commodities was achieved only with the emergence of industrial society." This quantum leap in reification, in which it came to represent an entire society's way of life, happened because instrumental reason repressed and eventually replaced classic Western notions of objective-substantial reason.

With a special intensity, Horkheimer—already in the 1940s—accentuates how instrumental reasoning, reification, and commodification take their toll on the natural environment.

> Nevertheless, nature is today more than ever conceived as a mere tool of man. It is the object of total exploitation that has no aim set by [objective-substantial] reason, and therefore no limit. Man's boundless imperialism is never satisfied. The dominion of the human race over the earth has no parallel in those epochs of natural history in which other animal species represented the highest forms of organic development. Their appetites were limited by the

> necessities of their physical existence. Indeed, man's ability to
> extend his power in two infinities, the microcosm and the uni-
> verse, does not arise directly from his own nature, but from the
> structure of society.[29]

Reification extends not only to the natural world and to social relationships, but also to the core of human subjectivity.

> Yet the more all nature is looked upon . . . as mere objects in
> relation to human subjects, the more is the once supposedly
> autonomous subject emptied of any content, until it finally
> becomes a mere name with nothing to denominate. The total
> transformation of each and every realm of being into a field
> of means leads to the liquidation of the subject who is supposed
> to use them. This gives modern industrial society its nihilistic
> aspect. Subjectivization, which exalts the subject, also dooms
> him.[30]

Do Horkheimer's own analyses lead him toward nihilism? Such a question
arises when reading statements like the following: "The theme of this time
is self-preservation, while there is no self to preserve."[31] In this regard,
Habermas notes, "Reason, once instrumentalized, has become assimilated
to power [that is, domination in the service of self-preservation] and has
thereby given up its critical power."[32]

The Transformation of Critique

Habermas knows, as an heir to critical social theory, that he must inquire
into the adequacy of this heritage. Do instrumental reason and reification
go, so to speak, all the way down? That is, are instrumental reason and reification so powerful, pervasive, and radical that no aspect of Western society
has escaped or can escape their demonic clutches? Is the barbarism total?
Lukács argued against total reification. He postulated a limit beyond which
reification could not go. But he did not offer a precise account of this limit.
Rather, he retreated to a Hegelian-Marxian philosophy of history. He spec-
ulated about a certain course of events: somehow, the proletariat would
chance upon an imaginary line in the sand, and it would spontaneously
come to consciousness about the economic causes of its exploitation. At
this historical moment, the proletariat would emerge as the supersubject of
world history. This proletarian supersubject would actualize a new world

history. By 1940, Horkheimer no longer maintained, as did Lukács, such a Hegelian-Marxian philosophy of history.

The Performative Contradiction of Total Critique

According to Horkheimer's post-1940 perspective, instrumental reason has always been the root, even the totality, of Western "reason."

> If one were to speak of a disease affecting reason, this disease should be understood not as having stricken reason at some historical moment, but as being inseparable from the nature of reason in civilization as we have known it so far. This disease of reason is that reason was born from man's urge to dominate nature, and the "recovery" depends on insight into the nature of the original disease, not on a cure of the latest symptoms. The true critique of reason will necessarily uncover the deepest layers of civilization and explore its earliest history. From the time when reason became the instrument for domination of human and extra-human nature by man—that is to say, from its very beginning—it has been frustrated in its own intention of discovering the truth.[33]

Habermas argues that this post-1940 perspective leaves Horkheimer in a disastrous conceptual conundrum.

> On the one hand, this reflection suggests *a concept of truth* that can be interpreted via the guiding idea of universal reconciliation, an emancipation of man through the resurrection of nature; a reason that pursues its aim of discovering truth will, "by being the instrument of reconciliation, be more than an instrument." On the other hand, Horkheimer and Adorno *can only suggest* this concept of truth; for if they wanted *to explicate* those determinations that, on their view, cannot inhere in instrumental reason, they would have to rely on a reason that is before reason (which was from the beginning instrumental).[34]

Briefly stated, Horkheimer's conundrum is that, in order to establish and substantiate the truth of his conviction (that all reasoning is instrumental), he must employ a form of (noninstrumental) rational analysis that he is convinced does not exist. This "performative contradiction"—the use of noninstrumental reason to demonstrate that noninstrumental reasoning cannot be accomplished—represents the conceptual dead end of

Horkheimer's turn to a totalistic critique of instrumental reason. Habermas writes: "Critique becomes total: it turns against reason as the foundation of its own analysis. The fact that the suspicion of ideology becomes total means that it opposes not only the ideological function of the bourgeois ideals, but rationality as such, thereby extending critique to the very *foundations* of an immanent critique of ideology."[35] Adorno was quite aware of this performative contradiction and was always consistent in it, but Horkheimer, Habermas contends, remained stymied by these conceptual difficulties since he was always the consummate philosopher.[36]

Nietzsche's Way

Habermas stresses that Nietzsche "points the way" for Horkheimer's total critique of reason. According to Nietzsche, reason is and always has been assimilated to and, thereby, domesticated by nothing but sheer power, sheer domination that only serves the subject's—Western society's—self-preservation. Habermas describes Nietzsche's position. "Reason is *nothing else* than power, than the will to power, which it [reason] so radiantly conceals."[37] Because Horkheimer and Adorno accepted this Nietzschean thesis of "the identity of domination and reason," as they put it, they could no longer look to reason in any form or in any location as a normative standard upon which to critique Western society.[38] Nor could they look to reason in any form to provide them with the right or the mandate to be prophetically critical. Where, then, would prophetic critique gain its normative bearings, indeed, its right and mandate to speak? Once Horkheimer and Adorno align themselves with Nietzsche's total critique of reason and abandon Horkheimer's original conviction, shared with Hegel and Marx, they must search for something to fill the role that "reason" had filled—the role of supplying the normative criteria and capacity from which critique gets its bearings. On this issue as well, Horkheimer and Adorno take their cue from Nietzsche.

Nietzsche looked to that which he perceived to be the opposite of reason, that is, to aesthetic appraisal. For this reason, Nietzsche portrayed both Socrates and Christ, the two classic Western figures who advocated belief in truth, as the "opponents . . . who negate the aesthetic values!"[39] By looking to aesthetic appraisal, Nietzsche, argues Habermas, "enthrones *taste,* the 'Yes and No of the palate.'"[40] For Nietzsche, *taste* takes over the position once occupied by reason, and *preference* takes over that of truth or knowledge. "He elevates the judgment of taste of the art critic into the model for [critical, prophetic] value judgment. . . . He reduces 'p is true' and 'h is right' . . . to simply evaluative statements by which we express value appraisals by which we state that we prefer the true to the false and good over evil. Thus, Nietzsche reinterprets validity claims into preferences. . . ."[41]

Habermas argues that, because Nietzsche supplanted truth with taste, he reduced critique to nothing more than "wanting to be different."[42] Nietzsche's only way of deciding which preferences deserve esteem and which do not remained tied to a concept of power that distinguishes between active and reactive force. But Nietzsche also knew that he could not have a concept or theory in the strict sense, because that would return him to the province of reason. He thereby based the distinction between active and reactive on *genealogy.*

> Nietzsche goes back to the very dimension of the myth of origins that permits a distinction which affects *all other* dimensions: What is *older* is *earlier* in the genealogical chain and the nearer to the origin. The more *primordial* is considered the more worthy of honor, the preferable, the more unspoiled, the purer: It is deemed better. *Derivation* and descent serve as criteria of rank. . . . Those forces with an earlier, more noble descent are the active, creative ones, whereas perverted will to power is expressed in the forces of later, lower, and reactive descent.[43]

Horkheimer and Adorno followed Nietzsche's aesthetic cue by nominating *mimesis* to take the place once occupied by reason.[44] Mimesis—imitation—is the capacity to perceive likenesses by means of empathy and to reproduce these likenesses by means of imitation. Specifically, mimesis perceives and reproduces resistances, rebellions, and the speechless accusations of instrumentalized and dominated nature, including the natural environment as well as human and social bodies. Habermas notes, however, that Horkheimer and Adorno could never "put forward a *theory* of mimesis" because, as was also the case with Nietzsche, that would return them to the soil of reason. They could speak of mimesis "only as they would about a piece of uncomprehended nature . . . as an 'impulse.'"[45] They gave up, therefore, on a critical theory of society. Having prescinded from giving reasons for their social critique, Horkheimer and Adorno could only practice simple determinate or strenuous negation on an ad hoc basis. "[S]o mimesis appears as sheer impulse, the exact antithesis of reason. The critique of instrumental reason can only denounce as tainted what it cannot explain in its taintedness."[46] Habermas's critique of Horkheimer and

Adorno's mode of criticism finds an echo in McCann's "oracular" criticism of Tillich's prophetism. We address this issue in chapters 4 and 6.

The Normative Basis of Critique

From Habermas's perspective, "the really problematic move" of Hork-heimer and Adorno after 1940 involves what they owed to Nietzsche: "[T]hey surrendered themselves to an uninhibited skepticism regarding reason instead of weighing the grounds that cast doubt on this skepticism itself."[47] Their "aesthetically inspired anarchism" of the 1940s, derived from Nietzsche, emerges eventually as "the idea of postmodernity."[48] As Habermas sees it, this approach, if carried out steadfastly, ironically would permit power as domination to advance and to exalt itself as the only propelling dynamism in history. Hence, nihilism. Habermas argues fiercely that the way out of nihilism's total skepticism and postmodern anarchy is through "the philosophical (not aesthetic) discourse of modernity."[49]

To avoid a trap in the performative contradiction of a totalistic critique of reason, thereby consuming the critical impulse altogether, then, argues Habermas, we must search out and scrutinize "the normative foundations" of criticism. He deems these moorings to be set "so deep" that they endure even the three historical developments that shook Horkheimer's confidence in reason during the 1940s. Habermas criticizes Horkheimer and Adorno because they "oversimplify [their] image of modernity so astoundingly" and do not "do justice to the rationality content of cultural modernity that was captured in bourgeois ideals (and also instrumentalized along with them)." He thinks that they overlook basic, though often repressed, liberative "achievements" of Western modernity. Their "oversimplified presentation fails to notice essential characteristics of cultural modernity." They share with Nietzsche "the same cramped optics that render one insensible to the traces and the existing forms of communicative rationality."[50] Like Sherlock Holmes, Habermas looks for where these traces and existing forms of communicative rationality dwell, often cryptically, within Western society. By doing so, he proposes to outline the normative bases on which the criticism of society might proceed.

Within the development of critical social theory we have witnessed the transformation of critique. We saw how Horkheimer took his original practice of immanent critique and expanded it into the critique of ideology.

We observed how he remade the critique of ideology into the critique of instrumental reason. Further, we noticed why, how, and with what result Horkheimer, along with Adorno, radicalized the critique of instrumental reason into totalized critique. Finally, we looked at Habermas's critique of performative contradiction and his proposed transformation of critique based on the normative grounds of communicative reason and action.

The relationship between the next two chapters is important. The more historical and sociological material, which I present in chapter 5, could be presented prior to the more theoretical and normative material, which I discuss in chapter 4. In fact, Habermas emphasizes that "existing forms of reason" in history and sociology precede his theoretical analyses.[51] I arrange my presentation, however, on a different basis. The more sociologically concrete material provides the more helpful entry into my final chapter. Therefore, chapter 4 investigates Habermas's theoretically oriented analysis of what constitutes communicative rationality and action. Habermas's theory helps us see why Horkheimer failed to find what he was looking for in the early 1930s and why, in the face of later historical disappointments, he abandoned his project of immanent critique. As we will see, Habermas, in order to avoid the idealistic shallowness of bourgeois ideals and the unexamined doctrine of progress in orthodox Marxist philosophy of history—both of which Horkheimer criticized—strives to root normative ideals deep in the communicative reasoning of everyday life. Chapter 5 probes Habermas's social and historical explanation of the rise of modern Western society in order to locate where communicative rationality and action have emerged. Chapters 4 and 5 also examine Habermas's focus on factors that repress and deform communicative reason and action. In this way, Habermas prepares critical social theory to befriend fragile existing forms of communicative reason and action so that they might gain strength, proliferate, and lead toward a more just, free, and unified society. Chapters 4 and 5 together represent Habermas's diagnosis of and prognosis for Western society in an age of globalization.

4

Theory:
The Theory of Communicative
Reason and Action

In chapter 3 we saw Habermas's dissatisfaction with the "cramped optics" through which Horkheimer and Adorno looked at the modern history of Western society. With these optics they could perceive in the West only one type of reason. Under the reign of instrumental reason, the reasoning subject always dominated its object—the other—by making this "object" into just one more tool for the subject's self-preservation. They turned to the mimetic capacity because it appeared to be the opposite of instrumental rationality. Habermas claims that even Adorno, however, "does not simply deny [to mimesis] any cognitive function." But "the rational core of mimetic achievements" could only be laid open to the extent that Horkheimer and Adorno could give up the paradigmatic optics they retained. Their point of view was "the paradigm of the philosophy of consciousness," also known as the philosophy of the subject. In this subject / object paradigm, a subject "represents objects and toils with them."[1] But when someone looked through the optics of the philosophy of the subject, one could not be sure that mimesis itself was anything but narcissism.[2] In fact, argues Habermas, if instrumental reason were as powerful as Horkheimer and Adorno claimed, what would prevent it from overpowering mimesis for narcissistic purposes? Still, observes Habermas, Adorno himself admitted on at least one occasion that not all situations could be instrumentalized. "The reconciled condition would not annex what is other, but would find its happiness in the fact that this other retains its distance and its difference within the permitted intimacy, that it remains beyond heterogeneity and sameness."[3]

Habermas repeatedly cites this passage as testimony that even the most pessimistic critic acknowledges that not all living space is instrumentalized. But after 1940, Adorno and Horkheimer maintained unrelentingly that thinking itself is dominated by "identity thinking"—what Habermas calls the philosophy of the subject—and this prohibited them from thinking deeply about Adorno's "reconciled condition." Habermas is not so inhibited. Referring to Adorno's statement, he proposes:

> Whoever meditates on this assertion [by Adorno] will become aware that the condition described, although never real, is still most intimate and familiar to us. It has the structure of a life together in communication that is free from coercion. We necessarily anticipate such a reality, at least formally, each time we want to speak what is true. The idea of truth, already implicit in the first sentence spoken, can be shaped only on the model of the idealized agreement aimed for in communication free from domination. To this extent, the truth of propositions is bound up with the intention of leading a genuine life. Critique lays claim to no more than what is implied in everyday discourse, but also to no less.[4]

Habermas aspires to reclaim this "condition," this "reality," this "life together" by fashioning a new set of optics, a new paradigm. This new approach is the theory of communicative reason and action. His purpose for thoughtfully reclaiming this life together in communication is that it may serve as a norm or criterion for social criticism and self-reflection. Before 1980, Habermas calls this purpose the "emancipatory interest," and it is inseparably linked to social suffering. The arduous road that Habermas takes with his theory of communicative action has as its ultimate purpose to contest social suffering. He makes this clear in an 1984 interview and, as readers, we will do well to keep this in mind.

> I cannot imagine any seriously critical social theory without an internal link to something like an emancipatory interest. That is such a big name! But what I mean is an attitude which is formed in the experience of suffering from something man-made, which can be abolished and should be abolished. This is not just a contingent value-postulate: that people want to get rid of certain sufferings. No, it is something so profoundly ingrained in the structure of human societies—the calling into question, and deepseated wish to throw off, relations which repress you without necessity—so intimately built into the reproduction of human life that I don't think it can be regarded as just a subjective attitude which may or may not guide this or that piece of scientific research. It is more.[5]

We begin the discussion by following Habermas as he locates the emergence of the philosophy of the subject. This entails identifying a crucial wrong turn that Georg Hegel and, later, both Karl Marx and Horkheimer took. Second, we outline the basic elements of the so-called linguistic turn in philosophical reflection that sets Habermas toward a new communicative paradigm. The linguistic turn brings into fuller relief significant contours of a noninstrumental life together that Adorno could only extol in a utopian sense. Finally, we delineate the key features of a communicative reason that serves as the normative basis of critique, as well as the standards for a new concept of social action. In this way we start to comprehend Habermas's analysis of modernity's deep problems and more hopeful possibilities. We can also begin to see the outline for a new, vigorous alliance of reason and the prophetic imagination.

The Modern Philosophy of the Subject

Habermas notes that, behind the philosophies of consciousness from René Descartes to Immanuel Kant and philosophies of idealism from Benedict Spinoza and Gottfried Leibnitz to Friedrich Schelling and Hegel, lies the conceptual model that he calls "the philosophy of the subject." This philosophical outlook takes as its paradigm the relation between a subject and an object, an "I" and an "it." According to the philosophy of the subject, an *object* is anything that can be represented as existing. A *subject* possesses two capacities. The first is an "objectivating attitude." That is, a subject can relate itself to the world, or to entities in the world, as if that world were an object. Second, a subject possesses, coterminous with this objectivating attitude, the capability to master these objects. That is, after picturing the world and entities in the world as objects, a subject gains control over them so that they serve the subject's interests.[6] A subject's reason, therefore, relates to these two "equiprimordial" capacities.[7] According to the philosophy of the subject, then, reason functions to *represent*—to know—objects as they are and/or to *produce*—to act on—objects as they should be in order to serve the subject's interests. These two capacities of reason—representation of and action upon objects—are, according to the philosophy of the subject, intertwined. "[K]nowledge of states of affairs [objects] is structurally related to the possibility of intervention in the world [of objects] as the totality of states of affairs; and successful action requires in turn knowledge of the causal nexus in which it intervenes."[8]

Hegel, Marx, and the Philosophy of the Subject

Hegel and Marx, especially in their mature and most influential formulations, remained captivated by this subject/object paradigm. Both, however, added a very important ingredient to the modern philosophy of the subject. The subject, they stated, exists as a self-forming historical project. The subject constitutes itself. In this way they departed from Descartes and Kant, for whom the subject exists prior to and thereby untouched by historical processes. According to Descartes and Kant, a subject is pure; a subject is unpolluted by the messiness of history and social conditioning. Not so for Hegel and Marx! They noted a dynamic that mediates between the objectivating-knowing subject and the acted upon, controlled, mastered, manipulated object. This dynamic constitutes the subject's self-forming or self-actualizing process. Habermas points out that Hegel and Marx borrowed this insight from Aristotle, who postulated that underlying all reality is the natural movement from potentiality to actuality. For Hegel and Marx, this meant that "the individual unfolds his essential [potential] powers through his own productive activity."[9]

Hegel and Marx both took this subject-object, self-formative model as the template for human social history. Humanity is itself a macrosubject. They conjectured that the human species mirrors the birth, growth, and development of an individual subject. According to the philosophy of the subject, an individual takes up an objectivating attitude toward the world it encounters. By accurately penetrating below the surface of objects and thereby knowing what really causes what, the individual subject can intervene in the causal connections. By intervening, the subject works upon and thus masters this world of objects in order to serve the interests of the subject. The subject's chief interest is its own self-formation—self-expression and self-actualization—as the way to self-preservation. In this way, the individual subject forms or actualizes itself as an acting subject by acting upon—by mastering and forming—the world of objects. The world of objects thereby bears the marks of the subject's own self.

In a like way, the human species forms itself as an acting subject-writ-large across history. Hegel put more emphasis on the representing, reflecting, knowing—idealist—macrosubject while Marx accented the acting, laboring, producing—materialist—macrosubject. Still, both employed the model of the self-formative, self-externalizing, self-creating subject-writ-large. Marx's claim to have been standing Hegel on his head retained some truth. But it is more true that Marx's praxis philosophy remained within the paradigm of the philosophy of the subject, though in a reversed mode. Further, within this paradigm reason, based on the model of subject-object relations, remains trapped as instrumental rationality.[10] There is another difference between Hegel and Marx. Hegel deemed the macrosubject of the sociohistorical process to be Spirit or God. Marx doubted this, having taken his cue from Hegel's student and atheistic critic, Ludwig Feuerbach. Marx regarded the human species itself to be the macrosubject of the world historical process.

Retrieving the Counterdiscourse in Modernity

Habermas affirms that the paradigm of the philosophy of the subject has been modernity's predominant philosophical discourse. He argues that the cramped optics of the philosophy of the subject prevents philosophers from perceiving other aspects of modernity. The same is true of postmoderns who have adopted the Nietzscheanly inspired, totalistic critique of reason. They see nothing else in modernity except the predominant philosophy of the subject because, ironically, they also remain hampered by the same cramped optics.

Habermas proposes a "counterreckoning."[11] Within modernity is a "counterdiscourse" to the predominant, modern discourse of the philosophy of the subject and its subject-centered reason. He detects an additional story line in the modern West. But it has too often been suppressed and at times nearly silenced by the story spun triumphantly by the philosophy of the subject, on the one hand, or bleakly by the so-called postmodern totalistic critique of reason, on the other. Without forgetting the real, social history of the West under the dominant and dreadful reign of the philosophy of the subject, Habermas discovers a suppressed story line that is also a real part of modernity. "[I]t behooves us to retrace the path of the philosophical discourse of modernity back to its starting point—in order to examine again the directions once suggested at the chief crossroads . . . [and in order to discern the] alternative paths they did *not* choose."[12] For our purposes we look only at Habermas's "return to the alternative that Hegel left in the lurch back at Jena."[13]

Hegel elucidated his mature philosophy of the subject as a self-formative historical process in his pathbreaking *Phenomenology of Spirit* (1807).[14] Historians of philosophy normally present Hegel's thinking and lecturing at the University of Jena in the four years prior to 1807 as a "preparatory stage for the *Phenomenology.*"[15] Habermas disagrees. "In contrast to this, I would like to present the thesis that in the two Jena lecture courses [1803–4 and 1805–6], Hegel offered a distinctive [in comparison with the 1807 *Phenomenology of Spirit*], systematic basis for the formative process of the Spirit, which he later abandoned." Habermas supports his interpretation with a close reading both of the Jena lectures and of the *Phenomenology of Spirit* and its aftermath.

Habermas grants that the main categories Hegel used to analyze human experience in both the Jena lectures and the *Phenomenology of Spirit* are very similar. In both, Hegel attempted to understand human experience by distinguishing among three basic types of experiences: language, labor (work), and moral interaction. Also in both, he analyzed what lies at the core of each type. But when in the 1807 *Phenomenology of Spirit* he set out to explain how these three separate kinds of experience are integrated, he proceeded differently than he had in his earlier Jena lectures.

In the *Phenomenology of Spirit* and thereafter, Hegel conceptualized these basic experiences as stages in the self-formative process of the macro-subject (Spirit). That is, Spirit reflects on itself, thereby knowing itself, only through a particular medium of experience. At one stage, Spirit utilizes language as its medium; at another stage, Spirit uses labor; at still another stage, Spirit co-opts moral relationships as the medium for self-reflection and self-actualization. Spirit unifies these divergent experiences by utilizing them as stage-specific media for a single self-formative process. From 1807 on, therefore, Hegel employed the optics of the philosophy of the subject to provide wholeness for human life.

Earlier, in the Jena lectures, Hegel had approached the three kinds of experiences differently. There he acknowledged that each kind of experience possesses an integrity of its own. Because of this integrity, these basic experiences cannot easily be instrumentalized and thereby used to accomplish some other purpose, even if that purpose were the subject's self-formation. Rather, Hegel envisioned a dialectical "interconnection" among the three kinds of experience, without reducing any to a means for accomplishing something else or as a stage to a more mature realization of self. The problem Hegel faced in the Jena lectures is the search for what integrates these separate experiences into a coherent life story. Initially, he located the unity of these basic experiences in the absolute identity of Spirit, that is, in culture and nature. He quickly became unconvinced that this romantic paradigm of reenchanting nature could unify the basic experiences, and he abandoned this approach.

Now we can see the conceptual problem that Habermas faces. Like Hegel in the Jena lectures, he acknowledges the integrity—the "equiprimordiality"—of each type of experience but he also recognizes the yearning for integration and unity among the three. Like Hegel, he also rejects the romantic paradigm. Habermas, however, unlike Hegel of the *Phenomenology of Spirit,* also repudiates the philosophy of the subject as the path toward the meaningful integration of life. He notes that Marx, too, thought that he was repudiating the Hegelian optics of the philosophy of the subject. Marx, like Habermas, remained indebted to Hegel's distinction between labor and interaction, or, as Marx put it, between the forces and the relations of production. Marx, however, argues Habermas, "reduces" interaction to labor.[16] For Marx, the only significant interaction is labor relations understood in a mechanistic, subject-acting-on-object manner. In this way, the optics of the philosophy of the subject is as influential in Marx's "materialist," producing subject as it is in Hegel's "idealist," thinking subject.[17] Habermas in two ways uses the insight that Hegel abandoned at Jena. First, he acknowledges the irreducible integrity of both labor and interaction. Second, he explores the experience of social interaction in order to lay open forthrightly the place and nature of language in relation to social interaction.

The Linguistic Turn

Habermas's search for an alternative paradigm to the optics of the philosophy of the subject, with its accompanying practices of instrumental reasoning and action, takes him on a journey through the linguistic turn in philosophy. As he travels this linguistic trail, he illuminates three landmark insights that contribute to the paradigm shift to the theory of communicative reason and action: Ludwig Wittgenstein's analysis of the connection between everyday language and social practice (or action); Hans-Georg Gadamer's inquiry into the necessity, nature, and significance of interpretation in reference to language and cultural traditions; and John Austin's and John Searle's conceptualization of speech as action-events, which I take up in the last section of this chapter.

Wittgenstein and Everyday Language

Wittgenstein noticed with particular clarity a close connection between language and everyday social behaviors or practices. In Wittgenstein's cate-

gories, this is the relation between a "language game" and a "form of life."
Initially, however, he did not think this way. In his first philosophical trea-
tise, *Tractatus Logico-Philosophicus* (1922), he tried to demonstrate, in the
spirit of the logical positivism with which he was associated, that only certain kinds of statements could be true.[18] True statements represent and thus
correspond to facts, and facts can themselves be proven using empirical,
scientific methods. Further, only statements capable of being true in this
empirically defined way are meaningful. All other statements that humans
utter are not so much false as meaningless, and even nonsense. People
could live life just as well, even better, without them. Both religious and
ethical utterances fall, therefore, within the realm of meaningless nonsense.
In 1922, Wittgenstein argued that true statements are true because they
reproduce a universal scientific language that stands as an ideal behind all
everyday languages. Meaningless statements fail to meet the conditions of
empirically proven correspondence to facts and, thereby, fail to embody the
ideal form of language.

Wittgenstein's early philosophy of language is, as Habermas observes,
"analogous in many respects" to Kant's philosophy of the subject.[19] As a
"pure subject" exists unaffected by the ordinary, concrete world, according
to Kant, so an "ideal language of facts," according to Wittgenstein, exists
unaffected by ordinary, concrete languages. Further, just as Kant conceptualized a subject according to its ability to know an object by representing it,
so the early Wittgenstein conceptualized language according to its ability to
represent facts. In 1922, Wittgenstein's notion of language revolved only
around its representational function, acknowledging no other dimensions.
The problem with this notion of language, as Wittgenstein himself came to
notice, is that it cannot account for his own philosophy of language.
According to his own thought, his philosophical account was meaningless
nonsense.[20]

Wittgenstein deliberately shifted the focus of his inquiry to real-life,
ordinary language in *Philosophical Investigations* (1959, published posthu-
mously). He discovered that in the grammar of every language—in a "language game"—resides a mode of living, a way of living together that he
called a "form of life."[21] For instance, within Jesus' language game of the
"coming kingdom" exists a "form of life" quite different from the "form of
life" embedded in the Pharisees' language game of the law. By noticing the
strong connection between a language game and a form of life, between
language and social practice, the later Wittgenstein no longer privileged

only the representational function of language. Here the social use of language or the "action character" of language—language "pragmatics"—comes into the foreground rather than the representational function.[22] "The medium of language does not facilitate first and foremost the description or affirmation of facts; it equally serves for giving commands, solving riddles, telling jokes, thinking, cursing, greeting, and praying."[23] Habermas takes Wittgenstein's insight regarding language pragmatics and, by refracting it through the speech-act theory of Austin and Searle, develops it into a shift away from the philosophy of the subject. Before discussing this proposal, we take up Habermas's basic criticism with the conceptualization of the later Wittgenstein. Habermas proffers this criticism in discussing Hans-Georg Gadamer's hermeneutics.

Gadamer and Hermeneutics

Wittgenstein's insight that a word's meaning is its use in ordinary language could be understood instrumentally. That is, a word has meaning only as a speaker uses it to act purposively on the audience. Such an instrumental concept of language is not what language pragmatics intends to bring to light, even though Wittgenstein's own formulations sometimes give that impression. Rather, language pragmatics illustrates how a language game embodies social practice, not merely the practice of a detached individual. When a person learns a language, that person learns a way of life; one becomes socialized or trained into a culture.[24] Through a language game, cultural tradition duplicates itself in the next generation. Further, Wittgenstein conceptualized each language game and, thereby, each cultural form of life, as a self-contained and reified monad. Each monadic language game remains closed to other language games. Only difference exists between each language game and, thus, between each cultural form of life. No translation is possible across language games and forms of life. Each is incommensurable to the other. Habermas describes this as "Wittgenstein's monadological conception" of language. The later Wittgenstein "remained positivistic enough to think of this training process as the reproduction of a fixed pattern, as though socialized individuals were wholly subsumed under their language and activities. The language congeals in his hands into an opaque oneness."[25] In actuality, argues Habermas, language spheres are not monadically sealed but porous, in relation both to what is outside and to what is inside.[26]

Habermas credits Gadamer's exposition of the "hermeneutic experience" for exploding the monadological conceptualization of language pragmatics.

Through the hermeneutic experience, ordinary languages show themselves to be neither a plurality of mutually closed monads, as in the late Wittgenstein, nor, as in the early Wittgenstein, a plurality of poor copies of a nonexistent ideal language. Habermas quotes Gadamer: "Hermeneutic experience is the corrective by means of which thinking reason escapes the prison of language, and it is itself constituted linguistically. . . ."[27] Gadamer focused on the act of translation in order to explain the hermeneutic experience. As Habermas notes, "[T]he trait that all traditional languages have in common and that guarantees their transcendent unity [is], namely, the fact that in principle they can all be translated into one another."[28] This potential for translation—this translatability trait—exists inherently in every ordinary language. Habermas refers to this trait as "the tendency to self-transcendence" and links it to reason.

Languages contain the potential for a rationality that expresses itself in the particularity of grammar. On the one hand, this rationality reflects the limits of the language's grammar but, on the other hand, this rationality simultaneously negates the limits of the rules' specificity. Reason, which is always bound up with language, is also always beyond language. Only by destroying the particularities of languages, the only way in which reason is embodied, does reason live in language. It can purge itself of the residue of one particularity, of course, only through the transition to particularities of another language.[29]

How does translation work? First, translation is called for in a problematic intersubjective situation. Seasoned translators recognize this fact above all. They do not reduce statements in one language to statements in another. Rather, they give full recognition to the strangeness of each language. Then, through a sometimes imperceptible, yet not arbitrary, exchange of views, they accomplish two tasks: assimilation and generation. They assimilate to one language what is foreign, thus enlarging and developing the language. Such assimilation begins to generate overlapping commonalities, common judgments, "an understanding."[30] Habermas, in agreement with Gadamer, focuses on these assimilative and generative powers of language.

Habermas notes, again in agreement with Gadamer, that the hermeneutic experience, which surfaces conspicuously in translation, also inheres in the interpretation and understanding that occur among speakers within a single language. "Translation is only the most extreme variant of an accomplishment on which every normal conversation depends."[31] The dynamics of translation happen *implicitly* in every conversation in which "under-standing" is reached. The implicitness of these dynamics allows them to recede, because, in true and trustworthy conversation, a basis of agreement exists. Wittgenstein overlooked these implicit dynamics and therefore con-ceptualized understanding as the mere recapitulation of a socialization process modeled along the lines of "training."[32]

Everyday conversation discloses its implicit translation dynamics, argue Gadamer and Habermas, when communication becomes problematic.[33] Wittgenstein thought that misunderstanding within an ordinary language meant that what one party or the other needed, perhaps what even both or all parties needed, was better "training" or more training or retraining into the given language game. In these ways, he thought, understanding would be accomplished as well as conformity with the form of life that the lan-guage game represents. Gadamer and Habermas do think that some kinds of misunderstanding—misunderstanding on the semantic level—can be addressed through "training." But—because they attend to the hermeneu-tic experience—they recognize a more profound problematic underlying misunderstanding, together with a more profound achievement in reach-ing understanding. Gadamer used the image of "horizon" to elucidate the hermeneutic experience of reaching understanding in ordinary language, and to illustrate the relationship between finite limits and the step-by-step transcending of present limits.

> A horizon is not a rigid frontier, but something that moves with one and invites one to advance further. . . . The horizon is the range of vision that includes everything that can be seen from a particular vantage point. Applying this to the thinking mind, we speak of narrowness of horizon, of the possible expansion of hori-zon, of opening up of new horizons, etc. . . . A person who has no horizon is a man who does not see far enough and hence overval-ues what is nearest to him. Contrariwise, to have an horizon means not to be limited to what is nearest, but to be able to see beyond it. A person who has a horizon knows the relative signifi-cance of everything within this horizon, as near or far, great or small.[34]

Habermas appreciates Gadamer's horizon image, which the latter appro-priated from Edmund Husserl, because it highlights the dialectical-dialog-ical core of ordinary language.

To the grammar of a language game belongs not only the fact that it defines a form of life [as Wittgenstein thought], but also that it defines a life form in relation to other life forms as one's own in contrast to those that are foreign. Because every world articulated in a language is a totality, the horizon of a language also includes what the language is not; the language shows itself as something particular among particulars. Consequently the limits of the world that it defines are not irrevocable. The dialectical confrontation of what is one's own with what is foreign leads, usually inconspicuously, to revisions.[35]

Gadamer conceptualized the conversational movement from misunderstanding to understanding as the "fusion of horizons."[36] The image emphasizes again how, in the hermeneutic experience, everyone exists as a participant. Indeed, participation is the indispensable condition for reaching understanding. A detached observer cannot come to a fusion of horizons, since such detachment prohibits the observer's horizon from being a part of the conversation. The vantage point of critical distance can never be better than taking part.

Gadamer employed the model of reaching understanding in conversation in order to elucidate "historical understanding" or, in other words, how tradition works. Gadamer set his goal very high. The Enlightenment, Gadamer argued, set out to discredit tradition and its authority in people's lives. By contrast, he pursued the "rehabilitation of authority and tradition."[37] In a famous passage, he noted: "And there is one prejudice of the enlightenment that is essential to it: the fundamental prejudice of the enlightenment is the prejudice against prejudice itself, which deprives tradition of its power."[38] Furthermore,

It is the general tendency of the enlightenment not to accept any authority and to decide everything before the judgment seat of reason. Thus the written tradition of Scripture, like any other historical document, cannot claim any absolute validity, but the possible truth of the tradition depends on the credibility that is assigned to it by reason. It is not tradition but reason that constitutes the ultimate source of all authority. What is written down is not necessarily true. We may have superior knowledge: this is the maxim with which the modern enlightenment approaches tradition and which ultimately leads it to undertake historical research. It makes the tradition as much an object of criticism as do the natural sciences the evidence of the senses.[39]

Habermas applauds Gadamer's criticism of the objectivism of historical approaches that treat a tradition and its textual embodiments as objects. Texts influence subsequent history. Gadamer called this "effective history."[40] Again Habermas agrees with Gadamer.

> For the history of the text's influence is only the chain of past interpretations through which the [present] interpreter's preunderstanding is objectively mediated with his object, even if this occurs without the interpreter's awareness. Historical events and documents that have been handed down do not acquire their "meaning," the descriptive comprehension of which is the aim of hermeneutic understanding, independently of the events and interpretations that follow them. The meaning is an aggregate of the meanings that are continuously sedimented as the result of new retrospective viewpoints. Thus the traditional meaning is in principle incomplete, that is, open to accretions derived from future retrospection. Historians and philosophers who reflect with a view to historical influence take into account the fact that the horizon of meaning cannot be closed off. They anticipate that the continuation of events will bring out new aspects of meaning in their objects.[41]

Gadamer's criticism of historical objectivism did not lead him, in contrast to the hermeneutical theory of the romantic era, to focus exclusively, or even primarily, on the authority of a text and the author's intention. Habermas quotes Gadamer approvingly:

> Every age has to understand a transmitted text in its own way, for the text is part of the whole of the tradition in which the age takes an objective interest and in which it seeks to understand itself. The actual meaning of the text, as it speaks to the interpreter, does not depend on the contingencies of the author and those whom he originally wrote for. At least it is not exhausted by them, for it is always partly determined also by the historical situation of the interpreter and hence by the totality of the objective course of history. . . . Not occasionally only, but always, the meaning of a text goes beyond its author. That is why understanding is not merely reproductive, but always productive as well.[42]

The interpretation of a tradition and its texts involves a hermeneutical circle leading to a fusion of past and present horizons. "We can decipher the parts of a text only if we anticipate an understanding, however, of the whole; and conversely, we can correct this anticipation only by explicating individual parts."[43] In agreement with Gadamer and quoting him, Habermas continues:

> The circle, then, is not formal in nature, it is neither subjective nor objective, but describes understanding as the interplay between the movement of tradition and the movement of the interpreter. The anticipation of meaning that governs our understanding of text is not an act of subjectivity, but proceeds from the common bond that links us to the tradition. But this common bond is constantly being developed in our relationship to tradition.[44]

The fusion of horizons between past and present is similar to that between partners in a conversation.

While Habermas finds Gadamer's non-objectivistic explication of historical hermeneutics impressive, he holds another of Gadamer's insights in even higher esteem. "I see Gadamer's real accomplishment as his demonstration [of] . . . the immanent connection between understanding and application. . . . By its very structure, hermeneutic understanding aims at gaining from traditions a possible action-oriented self-understanding for social groups and clarifying it."[45] Again, the relationship between understanding and action rises to prominence. Interpreters do not first form an interpretation and subsequently apply their interpretation to a situation that calls for action. On the contrary, Habermas notes in agreement with Gadamer that "interpretation is realized in its application."[46] Application in action remains a constitutive movement of interpretation. In this way, Habermas returns to the problematic of relating theory and practice, on which Horkheimer had focused decades earlier.

This is the core of "practical knowledge."[47] Practical knowledge is "global"; that is, it encompasses not only the goal to be reached but the means as well. Practical knowledge or reason "does not refer to particular goals that can be determined independently of the means of their realization. The goals that orient action are moments of the same life form (*bios*) as the pathways through which they can be realized. This life form is always a social life form that is developed through communicative action."[48] This indispensable connection between goals and means distinguishes practical knowledge from technical knowledge based on instrumental reason.

The Critique of Gadamer's Hermeneutics

Despite Habermas's considerable agreement with and even indebtedness to Gadamer, Habermas issues an incisive criticism. In the end, Gadamer's theory remained inadequate because it aimed to reestablish the "insuperable primacy" of tradition, that is, the dogmatic authority of tradition over rational argument.[49] Gadamer used hermeneutical insight into the prejudicial structure of understanding to rehabilitate prejudice. He saw no antithesis between the authority of tradition and reason.[50] Habermas argues that Gadamer maintained this perspective because he remained ensnared in the philosophy of the subject in its Hegelian form. He cites a revealing quotation from Gadamer that illustrates this ensnarement: "[This is] the aim of philosophical hermeneutics: its task is to move back along the path of Hegel's phenomenology of mind until we discover in all that is subjective the substantiality that determines it."[51]

Whatever truth that traditions embody, and Habermas does not doubt that they do, they also embody coercions, dominations, repressions, delusions, illusions, and so on. Habermas approvingly quotes colleague Albrecht Wellmer:

> The Enlightenment knew what hermeneutics forgets: that the "conversation" which, according to Gadamer, we "are" is also a nexus of force and for precisely that reason is not a conversation. . . . the claim of universality of the hermeneutical approach can be upheld only if one starts from the recognition that the context of tradition, as the locus of possible truth and real accord, is at the same time the locus of real falsehood and the persistent use of force.[52]

This recognition leads to reconsideration of the dialectical relation between tradition and reflection-reason. It means investigating a "situated reason" whose claims to validity are both context-dependent—immanent—and transcendent.[53] The concept of situated reason means that "the critical vantage-point can never be better than that of a partner in the communication."[54]

> Gadamer's prejudice in favor of the legitimacy of prejudices (or prejudgments) validated by tradition is in conflict with the power of reflection, which proves itself in its ability to reject the claim of traditions. Substantiality disintegrates in reflection, because the latter not only confirms but also breaks dogmatic forces. Author-

ity and knowledge do not converge. Certainly, knowledge [reflection] is rooted in actual tradition; it remains bound to contingent conditions. But reflection does not wear itself out on the facticity of traditional norms without leaving a trace. It is condemned to operate after the fact; but operating in retrospect, it unleashes retroactive power. We are not able to reflect back on internalized norms until we have first learned to follow them blindly through coercion imposed from without. But as reflection recalls that path of authority through which the grammars of language games were learned dogmatically as rules of worldview and action, authority can be stripped of that in it that was mere domination and dissolve into the less coercive force of insight and rational decision.

. . . The right of reflection requires that the hermeneutic approach limit itself. It requires a system of reference that transcends the context of tradition as such. Only then can tradition be criticized as well. But how is such a system of reference to be legitimated in turn except through the appropriation of tradition?[55]

Habermas pursues this last question by identifying a normative ideal and exploring a practical process for the reflective discernment of truth, on the one hand, and of delusion, on the other.

If understanding of meaning is not to remain indifferent to the idea of truth a fortiori, we must envisage, along with the concept of truth which measures itself against the idealized concurrence to be reached in unlimited and dominance-free communication, the structure of a corporate life in unconstrained communication. . . . In this respect, critical understanding of meaning necessarily demands the formal anticipation of right living.[56]

This is the task for a theory of communicative reason and action, which bursts the confines of the still-reigning philosophy of the subject and its notion of reason and action.

The Communicative Paradigm

With his theory of communicative reason and action, Habermas seeks to reconstruct the essential features of "a life together in communication free from domination."[57] He admits that such situations are never totally real, and yet, within the ordinariness of everyday living, people remain familiar with such a "genuine life." People necessarily anticipate the core features of this familiar situation every time they desire to be understood, that is, every time they want to speak what is true and to reach mutual understanding. But, in everyday situations of attempting to reach understanding, people usually anticipate these features implicitly rather than explicitly, subconsciously rather than consciously. Over their lives, speakers and hearers have gained a "know-how" of these core features, and this know-how becomes second nature. They have acquired and subsequently use this know-how without thinking about it. Habermas argues that these most basic features of mutual understanding, no matter how allusive, are radically cross-cultural, though he does not regularly use that term. He knows that many will question this cross-cultural claim and say that he is committing "the ethnocentric fallacy" by projecting "the prejudices of adult, white, well-educated, Western males of today."[58] He takes up the challenge.

Habermas aims to raise the implicit, core features of communication to an explicit "know-that." He seeks to know about the implicitly operating know-how of the core features. The usefulness of this "know-that" becomes significant, especially when the know-how of speakers and hearers in particular situations breaks down or becomes systematically repressed and, thus, distorted. This is Habermas's concern with Gadamer's explication of the sufficiency of hermeneutic understanding. By reconstructing the know-how for reaching understanding, he wants to identify the distortion of the know-how in order to heal the breach. By reconstructing the core features of communicative reason and action, Habermas hopes to nurture the concrete practices of communicative reason and action. The practices of communicative reason and action both depend on and transcend specific cultural and societal realities. Because the core features of communicative understanding are both immanent in and transcendent of social situations, they can transform distorted social situations.[59] "In fact, I think that the ground rules for public debate are only attempts to give a context-bound and historically specific articulation of an idea that is more widely shared, actually intuitively shared, by everybody who uses a natural language in one way, namely to come to a certain understanding with somebody else about something in the world."[60]

Speech as Action

In order to reconstruct the core features of the communicative know-how to reach understanding, Habermas commences with an insight first put forth by linguistic philosophers John Austin and John Searle. In developing a theory of speech-acts,[61] Austin and Searle expounded it as an alternative to the two then most prominent accounts of the nature of language: the theories of formal semantics and intentionalist semantics.[62] *Formal semantics* analyzed the semantic or grammatical structure of sentences. It also examined how grammatically structured sentences refer to or represent an external reality, on the one hand, and outside the sentence itself, on the other hand. *Intentionalist semantics* arose as a criticism of formal semantics and its bondage to empiricist objectivism. Intentionalist semantics studied first-person sentences in order to explain how a speaker represents and expresses inner, subjective intentions. By focusing on the intentionality of a speaker, intentionalist semantics allied itself with Edmund Husserl's phenomenology and showed kinship with Gadamer's hermeneutics. In distinction from both of these approaches, the theory of speech-acts focused on a different domain within the nature and task of language.

Austin noticed that when people speak to others, they actually "do things by saying something."[63] Formal semantics, as noted, focused on the grammatical and representational "saying" of an external-objective "something." Intentionalist semantics focused on the grammatical, representational, and expressivist "saying" of an internal-subjective-intentional "something." The theory of speech-*acts* focused on action. It focused on the "doing" that every saying-of-something, no matter whether the "something" is external or internal, performs on the hearer. Austin thereby highlighted the "double structure" of all speech as communication.

Speech "says" something—the locutionary or propositional function of speech—and it also "does" something—the illocutionary force or performative function of speech. The illocutionary-performative function generates an interpersonal relationship between speaker and hearers. For instance, "I warn you . . ." generates a different interpersonal relationship than "I promise you . . ." Furthermore, these interpersonal relations can vary, and often do, even when the representational-propositional content—for instance, "it's raining outside"—remains invariable. Finally, this illocutionary-performative capacity of speech "is built just as universally into the structure of speech" as the representational-propositional function.[64] Therefore, "communication in language can take place only when the participants, in communicating with one another about something, simultaneously enter upon two levels of communication—the level of intersubjectivity on which they take up interpersonal relations and level of propositional content."[65]

Habermas quickly points out that the performative-generative power of speech is often not uttered explicitly, but rather is implied. "[I]n speaking we can make either the interpersonal relation or the propositional content more centrally thematic."[66] This implicitness accounts for why linguistic theories before Austin, Searle, and Habermas did not analyze this crucial part of language. In ordinary speech, speakers often focus only on the propositional content—"it's raining outside"—and leave the performative-generative action or power of speech unattended, neglected, submerged, or even repressed. Sometimes, of course, speakers do this purposefully. These last possibilities can lead, though not necessarily, to forms of social domination and systematically distorted communication. Social domination and systematically distorted communication are momentous to a critical theory of society.

Habermas, while acknowledging the representational and expressive dimensions of speech, focuses on the illocutionary-performative, relationally generative (or distorting) power. Other approaches have competently explored and explained the locutionary-propositional-representational-expressive domains of speech but have neglected the illocutionary dimension. Because the illocutionary dimension is so determinative socially, it is "the most important [dimension of speech] for a critical theory of society that is a communicative theory."[67]

Habermas takes speech-act theory's insight about the ubiquitous, though often only implicit, generative power of speech and makes it his point of departure for his shift in paradigms. The philosophy of the subject had reduced reason and its capabilities to the propositional-representational dimension of speech. This reduction of reason meant that the relationally generative power of speech would always be an irrational force. This Habermas rejects.

The paradigm shift to communicative reason and action aspires to overcome the aegis of the philosophy of the subject and its reduction of reason by articulating a concept of rationality appropriate to the intersubjectively generative power of the illocutionary-performative function of speech. This is *communicative* reason. Communicative reason attains clarity by specifying the full scope of *claims to validity* that arise in communication. In this way we can see the full scope of reason.[68]

Reason and Claims to Validity

On the way to reaching understanding through communication, speakers unavoidably make four different kinds of claims on their hearers. Usually, one of the four claims takes prominence. Each of the four claims asserts that one aspect of the utterance is valid. Speakers embody all four claims to validity in the utterances that make up their communication. Hearers, likewise, in order to understand the speaker, require that each of the four claims be valid. Hearers, as Habermas likes to put it, take up yes or no relationships to the validity of the four claims. We consider this scenario one step at a time.

From the speaker's point of view, the four claims to validity are:

> *uttering* something understandably;
> giving the hearer *something* to understand;
> making *oneself* thereby understandable;
> coming to an understanding *with another person.*

Uttering something understandable is the claim to comprehensibility, which exists at the semantic and compositional level of sentences. Speakers must form sentences that follow the rules of a particular grammar and must put sentences together so that hearers can comprehend what they compose. The other three claims all presuppose this first claim. Once comprehensibility is fulfilled, it becomes the least interesting claim to critical social theory and to communicative reason and action. Habermas grants the comprehensibility claim and does not deal explicitly with it beyond that. The second claim—giving something to understand—is the claim to truth. When speakers give hearers something to understand, they speak the truth about a situation external to both speakers and hearers, so that hearers can share the speaker's knowledge. Making oneself understandable—the third claim—is the claim to truthfulness. By expressing internal intentions truthfully, speakers make themselves trustworthy. The fourth claim, coming to an understanding with another person, is the claim to "normative rightness."[69] In order that hearers may accept the utterance as valid and agree with speakers, speakers must choose an utterance that fits within the framework of social norms forming the background to the interpersonal situation. This fourth validity claim entails a close connection with the illocutionary-performative, relationally generative power of speech.[70]

Domains of Reality	Modes of Communication: Basic Attitudes	Validity Claims	General Functions of Speech
"The" World of External Nature	Cognitive: Objectivating Attitude	Truth	Representation of Facts
"Our" World of Society	Interactive: Conformative Attitude	Rightness	Establishment of Legitimate Inter-personal Relations
"My" World of Internal Nature	Expressive: Expressive Attitude	Truthfulness	Disclosure of Speaker's Subjectivity
Language	————	Compre-hensibility	————

Fig. 1. Four claims to validity and their contexts

[From Jürgen Habermas, *Communication and the Evolution of Society*, trans. T. McCarthy (Boston: Beacon Press, 1979), 68.]

The illocutionary-performative, relationally generative power of speech emerges more centrally when we consider which of the four validity claims speakers wish hearers to understand and thus to agree with. Habermas argues that the illocutionary component usually "determines the aspect of validity under which the speaker wants his utterance to be understood *first and foremost*."[71] Communication reaches its goal of understanding not merely when hearers understand the semantic, representational, and expressive dimensions of speech, but also, notably, when hearers say "yes" to the social relationship claimed by speakers. Reaching understanding unavoidably involves reaching socially normative agreement.[72] "The goal of coming to an understanding is to bring about an agreement that terminates in the intersubjective mutuality of (1) reciprocal understanding, (2) shared knowledge, (3) mutual trust, and (4) accord with one another."[73] The maximal meaning of *understanding* emerges with the combined rationality of all four validity claims.

Habermas argues that the illocutionary component of speech steers the pursuit of mutual understanding. It thereby carries a weightiness that makes it worthy of careful attention from speakers and hearers.

> The illocutionary forces constitute the knots in the network of communicative sociation; the illocutionary lexicon is, as it were, the sectional plane in which language and the institutional order of a society interpenetrate. This societal infrastructure of language is itself in flux; it varies in dependence on institutions and forms of life. But these variations *also* embody a linguistic creativity that gives new forms of expression to the innovative mastery of unforeseen situations.[74]

No wonder the illocutionary-performative component and the claim to normative rightness become the locus of heightened critical discernment. Here we have a fruitful communicative contribution to the prophetic imagination.

Systematically Distorted Communication

Habermas notes that if full agreement and maximum understanding were the usual, then a reconstruction—know-that—of the dynamics for bringing agreement would be unnecessary. Know-how would be enough. But "the typical states [of understanding] are in the gray areas in between [no agreement and full agreement]."[75] Crises in normative rightness involve one of two situations: when utterances do not fit with the normative background of a social form, and when the normative background of a social form is disturbed.

In much of ordinary life, people take a certain livable consensus about background social norms for granted. "If the investigations of the last decade [1970s] in socio-, ethno-, and psycholinguistics converge in any one respect, it is on the often and variously demonstrated point that the collective background and context of speakers and hearers determines interpretations of their explicit utterances to an extraordinarily high degree."[76] This determinative background possesses "remarkable features: It is an *implicit* knowledge that cannot be represented in a finite number of propositions; it is a *holistically structured* knowledge, the basic elements of which intrinsically define one another; and it is a knowledge that *does not stand at our disposal* [as a whole] inasmuch as we cannot make it conscious and place it in doubt as we please."[77]

When an utterance does not fit this normative background consensus, the claim of rightness becomes a problem. For example, if a speaker makes statements that either explicitly or implicitly fit in a parent-child situation, but the hearer is the speaker's spouse, then the hearer says no to the speaker's claim. The hearer can "problematize" the validity claim in one of two ways. In the first way to problematize in this example, the hearer contends that the speaker's parent-child social claim violates the background consensus of normative spouse-spouse relations. In this case, the hearer disputes the speaker's fit with the normative background. The speaker's misfit can be either open or latent strategic action. If the speaker's strategy is latent, two possibilities arise. One possibility is that the speaker deliberately attempts to deceive the hearer, which is manipulative communication. In the other case, the speaker's misfit with the background assumption results from self-deception, which is systematically distorted communication.[78]

But what if the normative background consensus in this situation equates the spouse-to-spouse social relation with a parent-child relationship? Then the speaker's social claim fits the background consensus, and the hearer's no must be directed to the normative background consensus itself. This is the second way to problematize the situation. In this case, the hearer's no creates a crisis situation of a different magnitude than the first situation. The hearer claims that the normative background consensus is itself "systematically distorted." That is, there is systemic deception that a consensus exists about the social norm. When a normative background consensus is systematically distorted, hearers and speakers have three alternatives: (1) switch to instrumental reason and strategic action; (2) break off communication altogether; or (3) recommence reason and action toward reaching understanding "at the level of argumentative speech."[79] Habermas often calls argumentative speech the level of "practical discourse."[80] Practical discourse is another important contribution for the retrieval and reformulation of the prophetic imagination.

Communicative Ethics

Reason and Argumentation

The purpose of the argumentative speech of practical discourse is to bestow normative validity on an utterance to the extent that its claim can be "redeemed." That is, speakers must give reasons to support the validity of a contested claim, and hearers must accept the reasons or supply other reasons

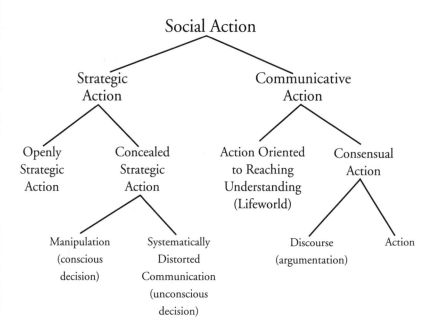

Fig. 2. Types of social action from communicative action to
systematically distorted communication

[From Jürgen Habermas, *The Theory of Communicative Action,* vol. 1: *Reason and the
Rationalization of Society,* trans. T. McCarthy (Boston: Beacon Press, 1984), 333.]

themselves. "It is part of understanding a sentence that we are capable of recognizing *grounds* [reasons] through which the *claim* that its truth conditions
are satisfied *could be redeemed.*"[81] Habermas states the idea more fully:

> The rationality inherent in this practice [of argumentation] is seen
> in the fact that a communicatively achieved agreement must be
> based *in the end* on reasons. And the rationality of those who par-
> ticipate in this communicative practice is determined by whether,
> if necessary, they could *under suitable circumstances,* provide rea-
> sons for their expressions. Thus the rationality proper to the com-
> municative practice of everyday life points to the practice of
> argumentation as a court of appeal that makes it possible to con-
> tinue communicative action with other means when disagree-
> ments can no longer be repaired with everyday routines and yet
> are not to be settled by the direct or strategic use of force. . . .
> [T]he concept of communicative rationality . . . can be adequately
> explicated only in terms of a theory of argumentation.[82]

The theory of argumentation lays bare the "suitable circumstances" for redeeming contested claims to validity when a hearer says no.

Argumentation is the type of speech in which a participant first pinpoints one or more of the four claims to validity that the participant thinks should be contested, and then attempts to criticize or vindicate the claim with reasons. Again, while each of the validity claims might need argumentation, a critical theory of society has particular interest in the validity—or truth—of social norms. An argument contains reasons or a chain of reasoning that is brought to bear on the contested normative claim, either to criticize or vindicate it. Participants measure the strength of an argument in a given context by the soundness of the reasons or chain of reasoning. Soundness means, among other things, the ability to convince participants to accept the validity or criticism of the claim's normative rightness. The soundness of the argument corresponds, one might say, to the rationality of the argument.

Habermas also talks about the rationality of the participants in an argument. Participants are rational or irrational according to the way they respond to reasons for or against claims to validity. Habermas even refers to the obligation toward this rationality.[83] Participants behave rationally when they are open to reasons, either by acknowledging the persuasiveness of reasons or by seeking to reply critically to reasons given by others. Further, participants act rationally when they manifest a threefold willingness to expose their own normative truth claims to the criticism of others, to redeem their exposed claims with reasons, if possible, and, if not, to be convinced regarding a contrary claim to validity. In other words, participants behave rationally when they learn through the argumentative process.

Arguments can be rational or not, participants can be rational or not, and the argumentative procedure itself can be rational or not. Habermas knows that many will vigorously contest this last point. He defends the statement by investigating the procedural rationality of argumentation itself and thus of "practical discourse." The most basic norms of argumentative procedure exist not at the level of what is "workable," no matter how important workability usually is. Rather, procedural norms of argumentation have the character of "transcendental constraints."[84] We come again to Habermas's method of reconstruction, of raising the implicit know-how of argumentation to the level of know-that. When we consider the procedural norms of moral argumentation, we encounter Habermas's proposal of communicative ethics.[85]

The core conditions of argumentative procedure are the reciprocity condition, the agreement condition, and the fallibilist condition. According to the *reciprocity condition,* all voices relevant to an argument's outcome get a hearing as full participants. Each has equal freedom in the reciprocity of raising and redeeming claims to moral truth. With the *agreement condition* comes, first, the provision that participants are truthful about their claims, criticisms, and agreements. Further, the agreement condition entails the exclusion of all coercion—physical, psychological, emotional, institutional, and so on—in reaching agreement about moral norms. Rather, "only the unforced force of the better argument" determines the yes and no responses of participants.[86] In this way, agreements "manifestly rely on the force of more or less good reasons as the only alternative to overt or covert violence."[87] Finally, the agreements reached concern the moral norm's foreseeable consequences and side effects. Habermas summarizes the reciprocity and agreement conditions as the rule of argumentation or the universalizability principle. "Every valid norm must satisfy the condition that the consequences and side effects its *general* observation can be anticipated to have for the satisfaction of the interests of *each* could be freely accepted by *all* affected (and be preferred to those of known alternative possibilities for regulation)."[88] Those who feel the consequences when a norm is operative ought to be full participants in the decision-making process leading to that norm. We can formulate the communicative ethics maxim in this way: consequence takers ought to be decision makers, just as decision makers ought to be consequence takers.[89]

The universalizability principle also rests upon the *fallibilist condition.* The fallibilist condition means that agreements about moral norms call forth future communicative testing. Fallibilism means the openness of every moral agreement to future confirmation and strengthening, or to critical correction, modification, and learning, or to overturning, redefinition, and new norm formation.[90] Because moral deliberations and agreements entail fallibility and, thus, provisionality, they always anticipate an "unlimited communication community," unlimited by social space or historical time.[91] This represents a significant meeting place for communicative ethics and Christian theology. At this point, Christian theology argues for an eschatological concept of truth.[92]

Identifying the three communicative conditions helps move Christian theology toward a communicative prophetic imagination that corrects the oracular temptation.

Pragmatic Expediency, Ethical Prudence, and Moral Justice

Habermas notes that "practical reasoning" can take up three types of tasks and that the character of practical reasoning changes depending on the task. He calls these tasks the pragmatic, the ethical, and the moral.[93] Examples of pragmatic tasks are what to do when the car breaks down, or when we get sick, or when we need money for a house. In these situations we make rational choices among pragmatic options for realizing a goal. Practical reasoning involves what is pragmatically expedient. In pragmatic situations, the goals themselves are not the issue. Habermas does not spend time investigating this form of practical reasoning, though he does not disparage it as such. It is essential in everyday life.

The other two forms of practical reasoning are more germane for delineating communicative ethics. What if the problem of sickness arises when returning to health is not possible, when, for instance, bone cancer sets in? In such a case, practical reasoning searches for an ethically prudent understanding of the good life. In this ethical task, practical reasoning commonly inquires into the person's cultural and religious heritage(s). This inquiry takes place because a person commonly has been formed to some extent through socialization into a community or communities of good character. These ethical situations arise commonly in life and often with significant gravity. Practical reasoning about ethical questions may incorporate many practices of communicative argumentation, but does not require the more universalizing features.

The moral task of practical reasoning commonly emerges when the ethical inclination of one community is compared with or conflicts with that of another community. At this point, the core conditions of communicative argumentation come into the foreground of practical reasoning. Here practical reasoning's task is to pursue the "morally right" or "morally just." Concerning the moral dimension of practical reasoning, Habermas identifies two complementary aspects: discourses of justification and discourses of application.[94] Discourses of justification concern situations in which features of the normative background consensus are disputed or have worn thin. At the heart of these features are the reciprocity condition, the agreement condition, and the fallibilist condition. These communicative basics are cross-cultural, a term that Habermas does not regularly use. When these basics are in dispute and in need of justification, they merit singular attention. Participants must overcome the pressure to address social norms tied closely to context. This does not imply that the more contextually situated social norms of ethical prudence are not significant. They are, especially when substantive conflicts arise. Conflicts of ethical prudence also result in discourses of justification, in which the three basic features of communication guide the deliberation.[95] When discourses of justification reach their goal, then a more context-sensitive discourse of "*application* of norms calls for argumentative clarification in its own right."[96] In many ways, discourses of application are the staple of everyday moral life. Habermas notes that discourses of application incorporate a principle of appropriateness to historical and social contexts and reflect on current motives, traditions, cultures, and existing institutions. It is not unusual, however, for deliberations about application again to make an issue of the most basic communicative conditions. In this way, discourses of application give occasion for discourses of justification. Habermas's thinking about these significant and complex issues also sets the stage for his sociological considerations, which we investigate in chapter 5.

Habermas's version of communicative ethics focuses on delineating the philosophical distinctions among pragmatic expedience, ethical prudence, and moral justice as well as on reconstructing the implicit procedures of moral justice in the face of ethical conflicts about the good. He does not himself, in his philosophical reflections about communicative ethics, enter specific discourses of application or address practical reasoning's task of ethical prudence. Philosophy and philosophers do not have control over specific outcomes in practical discourses. When discourses of justification and/or application are undertaken, philosophy and philosophers are no more than participants, which, to be sure, offers the best angle. "[P]hilosophy cannot arrogate to itself the task of finding answers to substantive questions of justice or of an authentic, unfailed life, for it properly belongs to participants."[97] This does not mean that philosophers do not participate in the most painful issues of the day. They do.[98]

Communicative Action and Strategic Action

Habermas embarks on a theory of communicative action to address the question of social action in general and the serious problem of coordinating action. Achieving understanding through language and coming to normative agreement through argumentation are the media for coordinating social action.[99] Habermas compares three models of action: instrumental action, strategic action, and communicative action. Both instrumental and strategic action are oriented toward success. When actors, whether as individuals or collectives, exercise instrumental and strategic action, they orient themselves solely toward attaining a subjectively formulated purpose. Further, they select means that they themselves deem appropriate in a given situation. Finally, they calculate other foreseeable consequences of the action as secondary effects—either costs or benefits—of their own success. These actions oriented toward success are "instrumental" action when the object that the action affects is a nonhuman or nonsocial entity like the natural environment. Actions oriented toward success are "strategic" action when the object that the action affects is a human, social entity. Strategic social action always has designs on its intended human, social objects. In this way, strategic action remains in bondage to the philosophy of the subject and to the social practices that correspond to this form of subjectivity.

The structure of communicative action looks quite different from instrumental and strategic types. Communicative action is oriented toward reaching normative agreement, because it proceeds from the core conditions presupposed in argumentative speech. In Habermas's proposal, communicative action entails reaching understanding and agreement as well as the social coordination or integration of action that flows from communicatively achieved agreements. Communicative action is always social action mediated through the integrative powers of argumentative speech.[100]

We have now familiarized ourselves with the core elements determining the paradigm shift to communicative action. In chapter 5, we take up Habermas's investigation into the history and emerging sociological shape of modern Western society. In this way, we see the theory of communicative reason and action as a critical proposal for diagnosing the contemporary situation. In chapter 6 we explore how the model of communicative reason and action helps refashion the Christian prophetic imagination after its oracular captivity to the philosophy of the subject.

5

Society:
Civil Society and
Deliberative Democracy

Habermas constructs his theory of communicative action as a critical theory of *society*. That is, communicative action is the norm for critically refashioning an already existing modern society. Therefore, his theory entails both a descriptive dimension of the society that exists and a normative dimension relative to the pathologies of the society and to its reform.[1] Further, he investigates the historical route that modern society has taken to reach its present form. Finally, he demonstrates that the communicative norms rooted in ordinary speech pragmatics have had historical effects. These effects have brought key emancipatory features of modern society into existence. To be sure, these features have often been dominated by other pathological, repressive features. Habermas undertakes these normative and descriptive tasks to overcome the "normative defeatism" that Horkheimer and Adorno exhibited due to the shallow roots of bourgeois ideals.[2]

I begin by sketching Habermas's account of Western society's transition to a modern society through the emergence of "the bourgeois public sphere." Second, I summarize his two-tiered concept of society, comprising the lifeworld and two great systems, the administrative state and the market economy. Here we examine Habermas's notion of the pathological "colonization of the lifeworld" brought on by the imperatives of instrumental and functional rationality and strategic action operating within the great systems. Third, I examine his proposal for a deliberative democracy that highlights the communicative possibilities of civil society as a political public sphere. Here we see the merging of his critical norm of communicative reason and action and his sociological prognosis for contemporary life together. In this portrait we find significant contributions for the Christian prophetic imagination in our time and place.

A Democratic Public Sphere

How is a democratic society possible and how might it thrive given the structural conditions of Western modernity? This question led Habermas already in 1962 to investigate an emerging democratic ethos that predated the liberal constitutional states associated with the American and French Revolutions. This democratic ethos arose during the same period that a new social space came about in Western societies. The structure of this new, liberal, or bourgeois public sphere stood in sharp contrast with the structure and ethos of the public spaces of medieval Europe, of the Renaissance, and of the absolutist monarchies of the seventeenth and eighteen centuries. While numerous sociological and historical differences existed across these eras and among ethnic groups, one feature united them. Habermas calls this feature "representative publicness."[3]

Representative Publicness

Habermas's notion of *representation* in "representative publicness" does not refer to an assembly of delegates who represent the ordinary people. Rather, representation refers to the capacity and ethos of the few, elite people of status—those who embody higher power, excellence, dignity, courtly virtue, or manner—to *present* themselves in *public.* They display themselves with their loftiness—whether riches, authority, culture, education, or birth—*before* the ordinary people in order to accentuate the gulf in status. As the commoners honor such grandeur through various modes of applause, they also recognize the shame that accompanies their own low status. This cultural dynamic of representative publicness remains the normative template overlaying events such as coronations, balls, high holy days, jousts, hunts, festivals, and so on. Think, for instance, about fairy tales like Cinderella. Historically speaking, the eroding of representative publicness as political culture began as the forms of display became more enclosed within the monarch's courtyard and perpetually off-limits to commoners. The development of early forms of capitalism progressively drove representative publicness deeper into the enclaves of royalty.

Early forms of capitalism were fully integrated into a feudal society organized around the status estates of aristocracy and peasantry. Gradually, notes Habermas, the early forms of finance and trade capitalism expanded, during the sixteenth century, into great fairs at the crossroads of long-distance trade. A twofold traffic in commodities and in news formed elements of the new commercial relationships, and this traffic began to unleash dynamics that eventually would dissolve a society deeply grounded in representative publicness. The traffic in commodities increasingly created horizontal economic dependencies among the merchants within the nonaristocratic estate. These horizontal economic dependencies gradually outweighed in importance the vertical economic dependencies that had accompanied representative publicness. Along with the increasing horizontal traffic in commodities arose the need for news about these commodities. Merchants benefited from news about the origin of commodities in distant lands and about the social, political, and religious events that influenced the production and distribution of these long-distance commodities, as well as events hindering such commodity traffic. Gradually, this traffic in news became regularized and institutionalized. Toward the end of the seventeenth century, this traffic in news broke beyond its initial reading audience of merchants to include a broader public.

The new horizontal commercial relations disclosed their transformative power in the mercantilist era of the sixteenth and seventeenth centuries in two ways. First, companies needed the protection of powerful "national" states with strong militaries, which needed to be funded. These modern nation-states financed these armies by introducing bureaucracies, which set up systems of taxation and revenue that remained separate from the financial holdings of the monarchs. These permanent bureaucracies and permanent standing armies became the new "public" state authorities. In this way, publicness departed further from the ethos of representative publicness practiced in the medieval, Renaissance, and monarchical courts. Second, the expansion of trade in raw materials produced in faraway places also led people to consider producing these raw materials domestically. The domestic arenas for such production, however, required more productive capacity than traditional single-household economies possessed. New corporations based in capitalist investment were formed. These new corporations were private, not in their location in a private household, but in that they were not organized under the public authority of the nation-state. Nevertheless, these private production enterprises bore significant public relevance. They brought into existence a new sphere that was neither the state nor household nor church, but "the economy." In the early nineteenth century, Hegel would call this private sphere the "civil society." Later in our exploration we see that Habermas's use of "civil society" forms a different category from Hegel's.

The great transformations of the mercantilist era were also accompanied by the "unique explosive power" of the press.[4] Not only did news itself become a commodity, but nation-states employed the press to promulgate new ordinances targeted toward private economic enterprises and the consuming choices of private households. In this way, the press systematically served the interests of the nation-state. The nation-states' use of the press, however, also brought one important, unintended consequence. Through the press, nation-states addressed a new audience and thereby called into existence a new public. This rising stratum differed from the commoners and from the older class that had emerged from the commoners, which included guild craftsmen—the butcher, the baker, and the candlestick maker—and shopkeepers. Under mercantilism, that once emergent, now older class began to suffer downward mobility. The new public addressed by the nation-state through the press are the bourgeois.

The Public Use of Reason

Two groups originally comprised this bourgeois audience: the educated (jurists, doctors, clergy, officers, professors, and scholars, including schoolteachers) and the capitalists (merchants, bankers, entrepreneurs, and manufacturers). "This stratum of 'bourgeois' was the real carrier of the public, which from the outset was a reading public. . . . In this stratum, which more than any other was affected *and* called upon by mercantilist policies, the state authorities evoked a resonance leading the *publicum,* the abstract counterpart of public authority, into an awareness of itself as the latter's opponent, that is, as the public of the now emerging *public sphere of civil society.*"[5] By using the press to promulgate its ordinances, the nation-state unintentionally transformed the private spheres of the economy and the household into a new public sphere. This transformation brought about a second momentous shift. While the nation-state employed the press for dissemination of information about its ordinances, it also, by creating this new public space of formerly private spheres, brought into this space a new audience.

This new audience quickly became a stratum of people unhappy with the ordinances. Ironically, this new public audience began to use the press itself as a "developing critical sphere." The nation-state had "provoked the critical judgment of a public making use of its reason."[6] This had begun already during the last third of the seventeenth century and developed momentum during the first half of the eighteenth century, particularly in

Great Britain. Critical reasoning made its way into the daily press through
the burgeoning gathering places: coffee houses in Britain, salons in France,
and table societies in Germany. Increasingly, the press itself became "a
forum in which the private people, come together to form a public, readied
themselves to compel authority to legitimate itself before public opinion.
The *publicum* developed into the public, the *subjectum* into the [reasoning]
subject, the receiver of regulations from above into the ruling authorities'
adversary." The demise of representative publicness as the preferred mode
of Western society was on the horizon.

> The bourgeois public sphere may be conceived above all as the
> sphere of private people come together as a public; they soon
> claimed the public sphere, [traditionally] regulated from above,
> against the authorities themselves, to engage them in debate over
> the general rules governing relations in the basically privatized but
> publicly relevant sphere of commodity exchange and social labor.
> The medium of this political confrontation was peculiar and with-
> out historical precedent: people's public use of their reason.[7]

The paradigm shift from representative publicness to the public's critical
use of reasoning closely matched the transformation of the press from an
outlet for merchant news to a place for debate of political opinion.[8]

In 1962, Habermas identified a third phase in the development of the
press: commercialization. "Only with the establishment of the bourgeois
constitutional state and the legalization of a political public sphere was the
press as a forum of rational-critical debate released from the pressure to take
sides ideologically; now it could abandon its polemical stance and concentrate on the profit opportunities for a commercial business."[9] The twentieth-century commercialization of the press mirrored another structural
transformation—the degeneration of the public sphere itself. The key
structural mode of the bourgeois public sphere, formation of political
opinion through the public use of reasoning, mutated in the twentieth century into a public sphere dominated by the systemic "practice of public
relations." In Habermas's judgment, the practice of public relations as a
dominant ethos of the bourgeois public sphere signals "a refeudalization of
the public sphere," in the sense of a return to representative publicness.

> Intelligent criticism of publicly discussed affairs gives way before a
> mood of conformity with publicly presented persons or personifi-
> cations; consent coincides with good will evoked by publicity.

Publicity once [during the heyday of the bourgeois public sphere] meant the exposure of political domination before the public use of reason; publicity now adds up the reactions of an uncommitted friendly disposition. In the measure that it is shaped by public relations, the public sphere of civil society again takes on feudal features. The "suppliers" display a showy pomp before customers ready to follow. Publicity imitates the kind of aura proper to the personal prestige and supernatural authority once bestowed by the kind of publicity involved in representation. . . . Because private enterprises evoke in their customers the idea that in their consumption decisions they act in their capacity as citizens, the state has to "address" its citizens like consumers. As a result, public authority too competes for publicity.[10]

In 1962, Habermas described this as a degenerative transition from a culture-debating public to a culture-consuming public.

Lifeworld and Systems

In the thirty-five years since Habermas wrote *The Structural Transformation of the Public Sphere,* he has reoriented his view of modern Western society. While remaining as convinced as ever about the significance of a critically reasoning, political public sphere for the future development of democracy, he admits that, in his 1962 pessimism over the prospects of democracy, he fell too much under the spell of the negative, totalistic critique of Horkheimer and Adorno. In 1962, the only alternative to Horkheimer and Adorno's pessimistic view of the liberal constitutional state was a proposed evolution of the social welfare state into a socialist state that would, in a totalistic fashion, take command of the market economy and its consumerist ethos. This was the proposal that Habermas's teacher, Wolfgang Abendroth, espoused and under whom Habermas wrote *The Structural Transformation of the Public Sphere.* Already in 1962, Habermas had doubts about this direction. By 1973, his doubts had become grave and led him to pursue a different view of modern Western society.[11]

In 1973, Habermas proposed a two-tiered view of society comprised of the *lifeworld,* on the one hand, and the mega-"systems" of the market economy and the administrative state, on the other hand.[12] Since 1987, he has also acknowledged a more pluralistically differentiated public use of reason than that implied in his 1962 study, which proposed a single bourgeois public sphere, specific to a single epoch and to a limited number of institutions.[13] Other movements, publics, and institutions, Habermas now acknowledges, make critical use of reason as a central feature (for example, religious publics; civil, social, and human rights movements; women's movements; working-class movements and institutions). His new openness toward these "autonomous public spheres" has led him to revise his sociological conception of modern society into a three-tiered concept. Autonomous public spheres with their medium of solidarity strive for normative influence on the political state with its medium of administrative power, and on the market economy with its medium of money.[14] We explore the implications of Habermas's three-tiered conceptualization after exploring the notions of lifeworld and system.

The Lifeworld

The distinction between lifeworld and system helps explain why Western society evolved into a "modern" society. The first key driver of modern social evolution is *rationalization,* understood through the paradigm of communicative reason. Communicative rationalization involves giving reasons in order to agree about the three basic validity claims, as noted in chapter 4. Habermas also refers to communicative rationalization as "linguistification."[15] The second key propellant is *differentiation,* an important concept in sociology. Differentiation happens when one social phenomenon becomes, over time, distinguishable from another social phenomenon with which it previously was fused as a single phenomenon. One might compare social differentiation to the biological concept of cell division, in which a single cell divides itself—differentiates—for instance, into an optical cell, an auditory cell, and an olfactory cell. Social differentiation produces a "division of labor." Differentiation as a kind of specialization helps accomplish different tasks more effectively. Habermas, following Max Weber, sees increasing differentiation as a hallmark of the development of the West into a modern society. The most fundamental differentiation in modern society lies between the lifeworld and the great systems of the market economy and the administrative state.[16] As we will see shortly, in modern society the lifeworld itself differentiates into three distinguishable, though complexly related, components.

The concept of a lifeworld involves the most common phenomena of human action. Two main features that help fashion action are the "situation" in which the action will take place and the lifeworld through which the action will be mediated. The situation stands out as a foreground for the action; the lifeworld exists as the background. As background, the lifeworld provides resources informing the action, but doing so implicitly and tacitly, at least at first glance. Components of the "situation" might include *spatial* elements, like a group of construction workers at a site with a grocery market a block away; *temporal* elements, like an upcoming coffee break; a *theme,* like refreshments for the break; a *goal,* like the purchase of drinks; a *plan,* like having the new guy go to the store. The action that happens depends on how the actors define and interpret the situation. Definition and interpretation happen through the background resources provided by the lifeworld. The theme, goal, and plan already give evidence of considerable interpretation. Such situations are defined through the resources provided by a complex network that makes up the lifeworld, which is always present and thereby preexists the action. The lifeworld is that part of the iceberg floating beneath the surface of every situation.

In modernity, the lifeworld itself has become differentiated into three distinguishable components: culture, society (understood in this instance as social groupings and institutions), and personality. The respective processes associated with these lifeworld components are cultural reproduction (the interpretation and transmission of cultural traditions from one generation to the next), social integration (the institutionalization and coordination of enduring, patterned practices of social action), and socialization (the experiences and the cognitive, linguistic, moral, and emotional competencies that make up personal identity). These different tasks intertwine in complex and varying ways. On an everyday level, these lifeworld components exist as a highly integrated narrative, as a life story.

In modern societies, communicative action spans the differentiated processes of the lifeworld. "Under the functional aspect of *mutual under-standing,* communicative action serves to transmit and renew cultural knowledge; under the aspect of *coordinating action,* it serves social integration and the establishment of solidarity; finally, under the aspect of *social-ization,* communicative action serves the formation of personal identities."[17] The lifeworld reproduces itself in each of its three components. Cultural reproduction and socialization reproduce themselves through great symbols, root metaphors, grand narratives, ritual, and life stories. Social integration reproduces itself through enduring social spaces and institutions in which patterns of relationships and action are normalized, regularized, and ritualized.

The lifeworld usually stands in the background in new situations, but in modernity it does not remain in the background. When faced by new situations, the lifeworld is always subject, at least implicitly, to testing.[18] To consider cultural reproduction, for instance, a cultural tradition always faces a test whether it adequately can define an external situation. In such testing of validity claims, communicative reasoning and action come into play. But the communicative testing involved in cultural reproduction often entails testing related claims about justice, membership in social groups, and personal identity and responsibility. Communicative testing of the lifeworld can confirm cultural traditions or can strengthen, renew, revise, or, in extreme cases, withdraw meaning from traditions. Communicative testing can stabilize social solidarities or it can renew, expand, or correct them; in extreme cases, it can disassemble social solidarities, leading to social anomie. Communicative testing can harmonize personal socialization and individual identity with collective identities or it can revise and develop personal identities. In extreme cases, communicative testing of personal identity can reveal pathological, alienated, or deviant identities. Communicative reason and action begets this rich complexity in the modern way of life.

Habermas offers two figures to help sort the complex ways in which each of the lifeworld's components (culture, society, and personality) intersects with each of the lifeworld's reproduction processes. Figure 3 (p. 110) depicts a healthy lifeworld. Figure 4 (p. 111) depicts the pathological disturbances within the lifeworld.

The Linguistification of the Sacred

Habermas conjectures that the lifeworld in the West has moved from sacred lifeworld to modern lifeworld. In traditionally religious, sacred societies, the lifeworld exists as a seamless, organic totality constituted, maintained, and reproduced through sacred myth, symbol, narrative, and ritual. Further, an aura surrounds these sacred elements, "an aura that simultaneously frightens and attracts, terrorizes and enchants."[19] Finally, at the core of sacred aura is noncriticizability, for sacred authority is immunized from full communicative argumentation.[20] Sacred authority, therefore, is sacred authoritarianism.

Structural components / Repro-duction process	Culture	Society	Personality
Cultural reproduction	Interpretive schemes fit for consensus ("valid knowledge")	Legitimations	Socialization patterns Educational goals
Social integration	Obligations	Legitimately ordered interpersonal relations	Social memberships
Socialization	Interpretive accomplishments	Motivations for actions that conform to norms	Interactive capabilities ("personal identity")

Fig. 3. Contributions of reproduction processes
and structural components

[From Jürgen Habermas, *The Theory of Communicative Action,* vol. 2: *Lifeworld and System,* trans. T. McCarthy (Boston: Beacon Press, 1988), 142.]

The differentiation of the lifeworld, together with the transition from sacred aura to the criticizable and redeemable validity claims of communicative reason and action, mark the modern "linguistification of the sacred."[21]

> By this [the linguistification of the sacred] I mean the transfer of cultural reproduction, social integration, and socialization from sacred foundations over to linguistic communication and action oriented to mutual understanding. To the extent that communicative action takes on central societal functions, the medium of language gets burdened with tasks of producing substantial con-

sensus. In other words, language no longer serves merely to *transmit* and actualize prelinguistically guaranteed agreements [as in sacred aura], but more and more to *bring about* rationally motivated agreements as well.[22]

Habermas also argues that the linguistification of the sacred brings about the liquefaction or the disintegration of the sacred and the increasing secularization of modern society.[23] Tillich's view of the mutual contributions of rational and prophetic offers a better way to view the relationship between the sacred and communicative reason and action than Habermas's thesis about secularization. Furthermore, the communicative contribution to the prophetic imagination is the way beyond Tillich's more oracular prophetism.

Structural components / Disturbances in the domain of	Culture	Society	Person	Dimension of evaluation
Cultural reproduction	Loss of meaning	Withdrawal of legitimation	Crisis in orientation and education	Rationality of knowledge
Social integration	Unsettling of collective identity	Anomie	Alienation	Solidarity of members
Socialization	Rupture of tradition	Withdrawal of motivation	Psycho-pathologies	Personal responsibility

Fig. 4. Manifestations of crisis when reproduction processes
are disturbed (pathologies)

[From Jürgen Habermas, *The Theory of Communicative Action*, vol. 2: *Lifeworld and System*, trans. T. McCarthy (Boston: Beacon Press, 1988), 143.]

Habermas proposes to replace the moral authoritarianism rooted in sacred aura with a communicatively conceived ethics appropriate for the modern lifeworld, discussed in chapter 4.[24] Thus, "[T]he further the structural components of the lifeworld and the processes that contribute to maintaining them get differentiated, the more interaction contexts come under conditions of rationally motivated mutual understanding, that is, of consensus formation that rests *in the end* on the authority of the better arguments."[25] In social evolution, differentiation within the lifeworld matches the emergence of communicative reasoning and action. Habermas does not think this happens merely in Western societies but that it is happening globally.[26]

Systems

In addition to and as a result of the differentiation within the lifeworld, a second type of differentiation occurs in the modern West. The lifeworld has always required a "material substratum" of food, clothing, housing, the production and distribution of other goods, protection, and the administration of and the settling of disputes concerning such materials.[27] Over the centuries these tasks of material reproduction have become more complex and thereby gradually have become uncoupled or detached from the lifeworld.

How did this uncoupling come about? The material substratum of the lifeworld has always depended on exchanges between people who produce material goods. In less complex situations, these exchanges happened through language, through which people coordinated their actions to produce goods. As the goods needed for the lifeworld became more diversified and as the production processes became more complex, these complexities overburdened the capacity of language to be the sole or even primary medium of production and exchange. A new medium was developed: money. As Habermas notes, coordinating action through language is always demanding. People must expend lots of energy in interpretation and communicative testing, and this leads to a high risk of disagreement. Money as the medium of coordinating material production reduces these demands and risks. It thereby leaves enough time and energy for material production itself, which the lifeworld requires. In addition, because money is efficient it frees more energy for the lifeworld tasks of cultural reproduction, social coordination, and socialization. Over time, money became the primary steering medium for producing the lifeworld's material substratum.

Eventually in modern society, two great systems—the market economy and the political state—uncoupled from the lifeworld. The breakthrough came with the institutionalization of money as a steering medium not only for the market economy but also for the state and the household.[28] The more complex the market economy and state became, the more provincial or irrelevant the lifeworld and its more face-to-face communicative moral reasoning and action became for anchoring the great systems.

Colonization of the Lifeworld

Habermas notes a certain irony in the social evolution toward a modern society. The communicative "rationalization of the lifeworld makes possible a heightening of systemic [economy and state] complexity, which becomes so hypertrophied that it unleashes system imperatives that burst the capacity of the lifeworld they instrumentalize."[29] Modernity's two great systems, because of the media of money in the economy and administrative power in the state, operate more and more according to the logic of instrumental-strategic action rather than communicative action. But, claims Habermas, these systems still need moral anchoring that cannot be provided by the instrumental-strategic rationality and action that characterize these systems. Instrumental-strategic action, mediated through money and power, always carries high levels of possible abuse, fraud, cheating, deceit, and so on—in a word, "mistrust."[30] The need for moral grounding to overcome these possible distortions is greater in the political state than in the economy, though without diminishing the latter need. Only through the institutional frameworks of constitutional and contract law, for instance, can confidence be created to sustain the market economy, mediated by money, and the political state, mediated by administrative power. In this way, we discover the necessity to recouple the economy and state with the lifeworld.[31]

Out of the lifeworld, particularly out of social integration, comes the genesis, development, and institutionalization of modern law.[32] Now we arrive at the theme of deliberative democracy with its bases in the political public sphere and civil society. Habermas notes two possible scenarios, and neither is historically inevitable or determined. In the first scenario, the great systems continue to emancipate themselves from the communicative moral resources of the lifeworld. In this case, the instrumental and strategic logic of money and power continues to invade the lifeworld, so that the systems increasingly colonize the lifeworld and inflict "structural violence" on the lifeworld's communicative moral reasoning and action.[33] In the second scenario, the lifeworld, with its communicative resources, develops itself so that it provides a vigorous moral milieu and accompanying institutions. Within these forms, the instrumental-strategic logic the systems need to produce the material substratum could function safely, that is, noncolonially. Habermas orients his critical theory of society toward promoting the second scenario. Growing deliberative democracy is the core of his proposal.

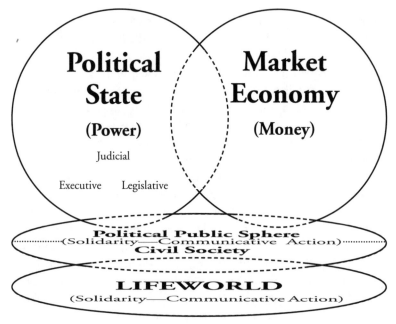

Fig. 5. Colonization of the lifeworld

Growing Deliberative Democracy

Habermas paints an elaborate portrait of a constitutionally based deliberative democracy. It incorporates the distribution of powers familiar in Western constitutions with their legislative, judiciary, and administrative branches. He justifies the distribution, however, differently from a more classical approach based on mechanistic premises. Not surprisingly, Habermas accounts for the different branches and for the relationship among them by the presence of instrumental-strategic reason and action or communicative reason, argumentation, and action in each.[34] For our purposes,

I confine this exploration to Habermas's desire to establish the moral moorings of the entire political process—that is, the three branches of government together with the political public sphere—in civil society. I do this because civil society harbors ampler possibilities—though not inevitabilities—for communicative reasoning, argumentation, and action.[35] As Habermas wrote in 1992:

> From that time on [1981] I have considered state apparatus and economy to be systemically integrated action fields that can no longer be transformed democratically from within, that is, be switched over to a political mode of integration, without damage to their proper systemic logic and therewith their ability to function. The abysmal collapse of state socialism has only confirmed this. Instead, radical democratization now aims for a shifting of forces within a "separation of powers" that itself is to be maintained in principle. The new equilibrium to be attained is not one between state powers but between different resources for societal integration. The goal is no longer to supersede an economic system having a capitalist life of its own and a system of domination having a bureaucratic life of its own but to erect a democratic dam against the colonializing *encroachment* of system imperatives on areas of the lifeworld. Therewith we have bid farewell to the notion of alienation and appropriation of objectified essentialist powers, whose place is in a philosophy of praxis. A radical-democratic change in the process of legitimation aims at a new balance between the forces of societal integration so that the social-integrative power of solidarity—the communicative force of production—can prevail over the powers of the other two control resources, i.e., money and administrative power, and therewith successfully assert the practically oriented demands of the lifeworld.[36]

Liberal and Republican Models of Democracy

Habermas distinguishes the discourse or communicative theory of deliberative democracy from the classic liberal (Lockean) and republican (communitarian) views of the democratic state. The foremost purpose of the democratic state in the liberal view, according to Habermas, is to safeguard and service a zone called *society.* Moreover, society is preeminently a system of economic, market, and labor relations, into which private persons entered freely and contractually. The liberal model defines citizenship primarily as the possession of negative rights. These rights are liberty from—and in this sense, against—the state and other citizens in order to pursue one's private economic and lifestyle choices. A citizen's positive political rights of participation have essentially the same purpose, that is, to give citizens the opportunity to assert their private interests in a collective way through the election of like-minded representatives. The liberal view construes law as that which makes it possible to define the system of rights, to discern which individuals are entitled to which rights, and to adjudicate the making and breaking of freely chosen contracts between private parties. The political process, according to the liberal model, is primarily a strategic struggle to control administrative and legislative power and to consolidate like-minded interests so as to maximize one's own interests. Finally, the liberal view desires constitutional procedures that favor the rational choices of private parties. Parties are favored according to their abilities to acquire their interests through legally strategic means. According to the liberal view, the constitution provides a framework for securing a free, contractual economic society that supposedly guarantees an essentially nonpolitical common good by satisfying personal plans and private expectations of happiness. The liberal model imagines the citizens' practice of self-determination as that of competing, private, individual subjects, analogous to the market economy.[37] The liberal model of the democratic state merely reflects on a political scale the philosophy of the subject in a privatized mode, which we explored in chapter 4.

The republican view holds that the foremost purpose of the democratic state is to bring about political practice in which the positive liberties of equally entitled, participating citizens are realized. The republican model portrays citizenship as the practice of self-determination by enfranchised citizens, who master themselves under the aegis of a common good present in a comprehensive, organic community. According to this view, law is the codification of an objective legal order; this legal order defines communal goods according to an ethical conception of the good life, which precedes the present body of citizens. The political process is preeminently a means of discovery or of coming to a self-understanding of the historically rooted ethical tradition, remains of the virtuous community that founded the state in the first place. In this way, the republican model envisions the virtuous community becoming institutionally realized in the state. The republican model can manifest itself across the political spectrum from right to left, as those terms are commonly understood. Finally, the republican view desires constitutional procedures that assure that virtuous constitutional guardians, usually in the judiciary, insure the integrity of the community. They provide these assurances even when common citizens fall short of the virtuous practices of political discovery and recovery of their communal heritage. The political participation of "fallen" citizens occurs in exceptional times of symbolic political remembrance, like bicentennial celebrations of the Declaration of Independence, and in episodic symbolic practices like pursuing constitutional amendments banning defamation of the flag. The republican model imagines the citizens' self-determination as that of a communal macrosubject—a subject writ large—coming to political realization as a harmonious, organic totality. The republican model of the democratic state reflects on a wide political scale the philosophy of the subject, examined in chapter 4.

Deliberative Democracy

Habermas's communicative imagination "reckons with [a] *higher-level intersubjectivity*" than possible within the philosophy of the subject.[38] The communicative model of deliberative democracy issues from communicative reasoning, argumentation, and action; it emerges in the everyday exercise of speech pragmatics. From this basis, deliberative democracy takes key elements from both the liberal and the republican models, roots these elements in everyday speech, and integrates them within the higher-level intersubjectivity of communicative realities rather than setting these elements at odds.

A communicative deliberative democracy, in agreement with the republican view, gives center stage to political formation of public opinion. This model differs from the liberal model's individualistic, private, market-oriented imagination. In this way, the communicative imagination "invests the democratic process with normative connotations stronger than those found in the liberal model but weaker than those found in the republican model."[39] Like the liberal model and unlike the republican model, however, a communicative, deliberative democracy also prioritizes the institutionalization of citizen rights and corresponding participation. This insures a broad enfranchisement of citizens for the political formation of public moral-ethical opinion. These rights and procedures specifically include procedures for how the state's lawmaking processes should be open to participation of the nongovernmental, political public sphere, with its vast, decentered pluralism, openness to civil society, and overlapping connection to the lifeworld.

By highlighting, in a sociological sense, both the political public sphere and civil society, Habermas corrects his focus during the 1970s and 1980s only on the economy and the state, with their media of money and administrative power, respectively. With this correction, Habermas now recognizes that constitutional states of deliberative democracy need a third great system, composed of the political public sphere and civil society, with their medium of solidarity, in order to thrive.

> The normative implications are obvious: the socially integrating force of solidarity, which can no longer be drawn solely from sources of communicative action [in the lifeworld], must develop through widely diversified and more or less autonomous public spheres, as well as through procedures of democratic opinion- and will-formation institutionalized within a constitutional framework. In addition, it should be able to hold its own against the two other mechanisms of social integration, money and administrative power.[40]

Political Public Sphere and Civil Society

Habermas develops an elaborate portrait of the "circulation of political power," comprising the constitutional state with its three branches, the political public sphere, civil society, and the lifeworld. Moreover, a constellation of "sluices" saturated in different quantities with communicative reasoning and action holds this circulation of power together.[41] For our purposes, we pare down Habermas's portrait to a sketch. He presents the political public sphere "as a communication structure rooted in the lifeworld through the associational network of civil society."[42] The political public sphere serves as a sounding board and warning system for societal problems that must be solved by the political state, because they cannot be solved elsewhere. Which problems the state addresses is, of course, an ongoing argument in the constellation of sociopolitical spaces. The political public sphere possesses unspecialized sensors for this purpose. It often detects and identifies problems by problematizing issues that seem to have been or have been settled. It also defines new problems in convincing and influential ways. Furthermore, it frequently furnishes possible solutions to problems and dramatizes both problems and solutions for the broad citizenship as well as for governmental branches. This last item is significant, because the political public sphere has a limited capacity *on its own* to accomplish the solutions that it proposes.

Habermas continues his portrait of the political public sphere as follows:

> The [political] public sphere is a social phenomenon just as elementary as action, actor, association, or collectivity, but it eludes the conventional sociological concepts of "social order." The [political] public sphere cannot be conceived as an institution and

certainly not as an organization. It is not even a framework of norms with differentiated competences and roles, membership regulations, and so on. Just as little does it represent a system; although it permits one to draw internal boundaries, outwardly it is characterized by open, permeable, and shifting horizons. The [political] public sphere can best be described as a network for communicating information and points of view (i.e., opinions expressing affirmative and negative attitudes); the streams of communication are, in the process, filtered and synthesized in such a way that they coalesce into bundles of topically specific *public* opinions. Like the lifeworld as a whole, so, too, the [political] public sphere is reproduced through communicative action, for which mastery of a natural language suffices; it is tailored to the *general comprehensibility* of everyday communicative practice. We have become acquainted with the "lifeworld" as a reservoir for simple interactions: specialized systems of action and knowledge that are differentiated within the lifeworld remain tied to these interactions. These systems fall into one of two categories. Systems like religion, education, and the family become associated with general reproductive functions of the lifeworld (that is, with cultural reproduction, social integration, or socialization). Systems like science, morality, and art take up different validity aspects of everyday communicative action (truth, rightness, or veracity). The [political] public sphere, however, is specialized in neither of these two ways; to the extent that it extends to politically relevant questions, it leaves their specialized treatment to the political system. Rather, the [political] public sphere distinguishes itself through a *communication structure* that is related to a third feature of communicative action: it refers neither to the *functions* nor to the *contents* of everyday communication but to the *social space* generated in communicative action.[43]

By portraying the political public sphere in this way, Habermas accentuates the "architectural metaphors" that provide us the sociological imagination to know what we are talking about when we say "political public sphere." And so we speak of forums, arenas, stages, and so on, and of assemblies, presentations, and performances. The political public sphere doggedly accompanies the concrete locales where audiences physically gather. But the political public sphere also expands beyond these physical locales. This expansion happens when these forums and arenas detach from their physical spaces and extend through various media to scattered readers, listeners, and viewers. The vigor of the political public sphere, therefore, depends on both the physical and virtual dimensions.[44]

Habermas analyzes other aspects of the political public sphere that, given our limited scope, we can only mention. Some aspects relate to the internal dynamics of the political public sphere, while others relate to the political public sphere's connections to the megasystems of the state and economy, as well as to the lifeworld. Habermas scrutinizes the political public sphere's orientation to citizen laypersons and how this lay orientation relates to the political expertise in governmental branches. This lay orientation relieves the communicative reasoning of the political public sphere from legal decision making in the precise sense, which is reserved for constitutionally instituted state processes. This release of burden permits lay citizenship to engage in the significant and strenuous work of forming public opinion rooted in communicative reasoning and argumentation. Moreover, Habermas vigilantly distinguishes the communicative formation of political public opinion from statistical surveying and poll taking. Another vital consideration is both the scope and quality of available public media. Finally, the quality, legitimacy, and measure of influence of the political public sphere on state processes across its branches remain critical.

While focusing on the political public sphere's internal dynamics and on its external connections with the state, Habermas likewise focuses on its relationship with the lifeworld.

> The political public sphere can fulfill its function of perceiving and thematizing encompassing social problems only insofar as it develops out of the communication taking place among *those who are potentially affected.* It is carried by a public recruited from the entire citizenry. But in the diverse voices of this public, one hears the echo of private experiences that are caused throughout society by the externalities (and internal disturbances) of various functional systems [like the market economy]—and even by the very state apparatus on whose regulatory activities the complex and poorly coordinated subsystems depend. Systemic deficiencies are experienced in the context of individual life histories; such burdens accumulate in the lifeworld. The latter has the appropriate antennae, for in its horizon are intermeshed the private life histories of the "clients" of functional systems that might be failing in their delivery of services. It is only for those who are immediately affected that such services are paid in the currency of "use values." Besides religion, art, and literature, only the spheres of "private" life have an existential language at their disposal, in which such socially generated problems can be *assessed in terms of one's own life history.* Problems voiced in the [political] public sphere first become visible when they are mirrored in personal life experi-

ences. To the extent that these experiences find their concise expression in the languages of religion, art, and literature, the "literary" public sphere in the broader sense, which is specialized for the articulation of values and world disclosure, is intertwined with the political public sphere.[45]

The connection between the political public sphere and the lifeworld not only shows where Habermas positions religion, which we consider in chapter 6, but also the key role that civil society plays. We turn now to describe and, if possible, to define civil society.

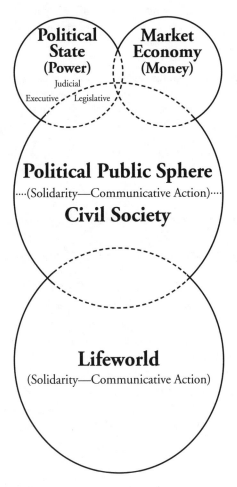

Fig. 6. Deliberative democracy and communicative imagination

Civil society arises from the thick network of life histories grounded in the private lives and lifeworld of citizens. It is a vast and pluralistic institutional threshold that emerges unpredictably from the lifeworld. It emerges when personal life histories mesh with other life histories while sharing and processing the moral wisdom rooted in the lifeworld. This is civil society's internal relationship with the lifeworld. Externally, as a threshold, institutions of civil society function as a "sluice" for the flow of moral wisdom. Such wisdom issues from the lifeworld into the political public sphere to form public opinion. In this way, civil society and the political public sphere form a two-sided threshold between the megasystems of the state and economy, on the one hand, and the lifeworld, on the other. Institutions of civil society, therefore, "form the organizational substratum of the general public of citizens."[46]

> Civil society is composed of those more or less spontaneously emergent associations, organizations, and movements that, attuned to how societal problems resonate in the private life spheres, distill and transmit such reactions in amplified form to the [political] public sphere. The core of civil society comprises a network of associations that institutionalizes problem-solving discourses on questions of general interest inside the framework of organized public spheres.[47]

The interlocking network of basic constitutional rights—of religion, speech, and association—is a necessary, though not sufficient, condition for the operation of civil society as well as the political public sphere. We can see this clearly, notes Habermas, by contrasting constitutional democracies with the totalitarian societies of bureaucratic socialism. A vibrant civil society in collaboration with the political public sphere provides the best assurance that the branches of the constitutional state will protect, expand, strengthen, and promote these constitutional rights. A second condition is necessary for a thriving civil society: a strong communicative ethos.[48] We examine this last issue in chapter 6. Habermas offers a normative description of how these sociological phenomena "ought" to work in order for a deliberative democracy to thrive and endure. To be sure, this normative description stands in tension with empirical accounts. Like Habermas, we stand "between facts and norms."[49]

PART THREE

Prophetic Reason and Communicative Imagination

6

Civil Society and Congregations as Prophetic Public Companions

Christian theology, on numerous issues and in various ways, has engaged critical social theory and Habermas's communicative turn. In this last chapter we consider the interaction of critical social theory and Christian imagination from one angle: how can the communicative turn in critical social theory work with the prophetic imagination to emerge in Christian congregations in North America? The motivation for this undertaking comes from Tillich, who explored the mutual contributions between prophetic and rational criticisms, and who suggested the congregation as the Protestant form of grace. First, chapter 6 harvests insights from previous chapters, gathering them to help Christian imagination. Second, this chapter imagines communicatively prophetic reason practiced in emerging missional congregations. In this way we retrieve and refashion the prophetic imagination for the critically normative speech and action that deliberative democracies desperately need.

Harvesting the Fruits of Our Inquiry

Horkheimer and the Idea of Critical Social Theory

First, Horkheimer persuasively analyzes the bankruptcy that the traditional theory of the previous era had reached. The nadir of this bankruptcy came about under positivism and its uncritical alliance with the way things are, with the social, economic, and political status quo of the bourgeois era. With the influential assistance of positivistic philosophy and especially positivistic science, with its aura of success and progress, the tepid veneer of the bourgeois era made society inattentive toward internal social contradictions that reversed gains of the Enlightenment. "A return to barbarism is always open."[1] By the early 1930s this was happening in Germany and spreading aggressively across Europe under Hitler's leadership. Prophetic imagination rejects positivism and sees it coming even in sheep's clothing.

Second, Horkheimer calls for a "*critical* theory" with "a sharp eye for misery and injustice."[2] Against his less rational hero Arthur Schopenhauer, Horkheimer insists that the critical theory of society be based in reason, but, for two reasons, not in reason in the Kantian or even neo-Kantian fashion. The Kantian notion of reason is transcendentally based and thereby remains abstract. That is, transcendental reason is abstracted from and aloof from real history and therefore from everyday suffering and injustice. Second, the Kantian notion of reason is always located individually and, therefore, has no direct connection to social realities and to the social sources of suffering. Therefore, social realities, like the state and the economy, do not proceed from rational norms. Rather, they act like mechanisms, like machines that respond to the push of different forces and powers. The Kantian or neo-Kantian scenario envisions individuals, even if each were connected atomistically to a rational source of norms and justice, who are merely objects of the machinelike realities of the state and economy. Understood this way, individuals are cogs in the machine of grand social realities, functionaries of social organisms that act according to arational, or even irrational, natural impulses or appetites. Individuals are body parts that, like zombies, obey a mindless command center.

Third, Horkheimer searches for a new understanding of reason by harvesting Hegel's insight into the dialectical nature of history. Reason itself is implicated in the dialectically developmental movements of history. Hegel refuted the idea that reason—and truth—is outside the dynamics of history and, in this sense, objective and ahistorical. Reason—and truth—is not some hypostatized, frozen object immune from the flux of time and everyday life. Individuals, therefore, do not through their history merely draw closer to or distance themselves from an imagined ahistorical truth. Rather, a key characteristic of truth and reason is permeation by time and historical flux. Truth and reason and the dynamics of history mutually condition each other. "It is of the very essence of authentic knowledge [truth and reason] never to be settled once and for all."[3] Prophetic imagination pursues a critical theory of reason coupled with an eschatological understanding of history. In this way, the doctrine of creation permeates prophetic imagination and authorizes prophetic reasoning.

Fourth, Horkheimer inaugurates a "critical *theory*" that incorporates materialist sensibilities. With Horkheimer, prophetic imagination seeks the insights of hybrid approaches. Critical theories existed before Horkheimer, as he is well aware. But they focused too narrowly on cognitive, epistemological issues, remaining divorced from the social conditioning and consequences of cognition. A critical theory of material matters brings both social conditioning and consequences into prophetic reasoning. Prophetic reasoning depends on this perspective to keep a sharp eye on social misery and injustice.

Fifth, Horkheimer's pursuit of social norms in criticism of the status quo leads him to take up immanent critique. Immanent critique excavates the founding ideas and documents of a social reality, like Western Enlightenment civilization, for the norms and ideals that gave it birth. Immanent critique often must retrieve norms and ideals that have been forgotten or repressed, usually because they inconvenience a social class or social arrangement. It then holds the reigning society accountable to its own normative standards and suggests reforms that will bring conformity to its original ideals. For instance, Martin Luther King Jr.'s "I Have a Dream" speech is a paradigmatic instance of immanent critique, especially when we view the speech and nonviolent direct action within the judicial and legislative enactments of civil rights. King's "Letter from Birmingham Jail" represents immanent critique of the moderate-liberal biblical religion existing in the American South in 1963.

Sixth, Horkheimer discovers the limitations of immanent critique and the necessity, therefore, to take up another project, the critique of ideology. Immanent critique assumes preeminently that the historical-social process that produced suffering and injustice is a departure from original norms and ideals. Given this assumption, the major tasks of immanent critique are retrieval and return. The critique of ideology makes a different assumption. It is more suspicious. It suspects that the status quo of social suffering and injustice does not come about merely because of a *departure* from original norms and ideals that are themselves true and rational. Rather, the critique of ideology investigates how the status quo exists as the authentic historical *outgrowth* of norms and ideals that have always been false.

Prophetic reasoning hones different skills when this is the situation. Ideology is a well-crafted, coherent narrative that highlights norms and ideals that seem right—and that might even be right when considered abstractly — in order to justify social arrangements that produce suffering and injustice. All the while ideology parades the—abstract—rightness of its norms and ideals. Prophetic reasoning, in addressing ideology, no longer retrieves and reforms but exposes. The critique of ideology attends to "the historical use of truth as an instrument of power" and researches the historical origins of an ideological discourse to unmask "an alliance between [so-called] truth and ascending classes."[4] The critique of ideology fine-tunes itself to class interests and the subservience of norms and values to the interests of dominant economic classes. It suspects, therefore, that the false norms and values of an ideological narrative have deeper roots than the ill intentions of certain *individuals*. Rather, a false *social* or *collective* consciousness arises over time, usually in both dominant and oppressed classes. False consciousness exists about the truth and rationality of an ideology's norms and ideals as well as about the causal linkage between the reigning ideology and the production and maintenance of class suffering and injustice. Not surprisingly, even oppressed classes might extol the ideological narrative that produces and sustains their suffering. Furthermore, false consciousness frequently produces in oppressed classes a vehement self-loathing for failing to live up to an ideology's norms and ideals, for failing to achieve.[5] Horkheimer borrows this crucial insight from Freud's early work. If even the oppressed classes internalize the so-called truth and rationality of an ideological narrative, who is in a position and has the critical capabilities to see through the charade? Who, finally, will be the agent of liberation?

Seventh, these questions trouble Horkheimer and lead him to abandon his romantic notions of oppressed peoples. He realizes that the oppressed classes cannot unmask and liberate themselves from the ideological cloak that produces and sustains suffering and injustice. This is the fruit of Freud's insight coupled with the failure of Marxism in the Soviet Union. Horkheimer departs from Marxist materialism in the orthodox sense, which viewed the oppressed classes as the leading agents of their own liberation—"workers of the world unite." Here, too, critical social theory makes a significant contribution to the prophetic imagination and prophetic reasoning.

Eighth, Horkheimer inaugurates a search for a new emancipatory agent. Here we have his own brand of critical theory. Critical theorists, Horkheimer states, are themselves the crucial agents of liberation, the vanguard class. And theory is the critical and liberative practice with which theorists bring about a true and just social situation. With this insight, the Frankfurt School develops an integrity of its own, so to speak. The situation in Germany will turn deeply tragic and demonic so quickly that Horkheimer will have no time to deepen this new turn. Even if he had had time, one wonders how long he would have regarded theorists alone as the emancipatory agents of a rational society. Soon, anyway, he and Adorno forsook critical theory as a theory of truth and reason. Tillich's theology of prophetic reason contests that reason should be forsaken.

Tillich and the Theology of Prophetic Reasoning

First, Tillich recognizes that Christian theology holds within itself warrants for rational criticism. That is, the tenets of Christian theology make rational criticism a legitimate discipline in which to engage. The Christian theological authorization to practice rational criticism pertains to theologians and nontheologians. Further, Christian theology warrants rational criticism for non-Christians or for those not seeking Christian theological warrants. With this argument in 1929, Tillich distinguishes himself from Karl Barth's dialectical theology. Tillich's self-distinction is historically important because, earlier, Barth and Tillich had often been yoked and, indeed, had yoked themselves on many issues of common importance. Tillich's self-distinction on this score is systematically important, because in it we perceive basic differences ranging across issues that lie beyond the scope of this inquiry. For our purposes, Tillich's reflections offer Christian theology the initial warrants to engage critical social theory as a companion for the prophetic imagination.

Second, Tillich ascertains the reciprocal contributions of rational analytic insight and prophetic depth. The divine prophetic depth of rational insight prevents rational criticism from becoming reactionary and fanatical, on the one hand, and from becoming contingent on the standpoint, opinion, and mood of rational critics, on the other hand. Contingent criticism results finally in relativism and nihilism. These effects damage, even destroy, the seriousness, the compelling quality, and the hopefulness of truth and justice, and they abandon real history and society to the arbitrary will of the powerful. The prophetic depth of reason means that God aspires to reroot reason in the divine. Prophetic depth contests the totalistic reduction of reason to power as demonic domination as well as the temptation to abandon rational analysis and insight as if the demonic had already gained domination. Indeed, prophetic depth obligates rational criticism to attend vigilantly to actual cases in which reason acquiesces to power, in the knowledge that the seeming triumph of evil in human and earthwide suffering remains, nevertheless, partial and not total.

Rational criticism contributes to prophetic critique the particularity and disciplined closeness of reasoned analytic scrutiny. It strives to uncover real social and historical colonizations of reason and, despite the pervasiveness of colonization, offers possible reconstructions of a more just and true, more rational society. In order for rational criticism to make this contribution, it requires a dialectic of reason of the sort offered by Habermas, as noted in chapter 4. Rational criticism's disciplined concreteness contests the temptation of prophetic criticism to become abstract. Left to itself, such abstraction incubates a kind of prophetic—false to be sure—self-justifying heroism that instrumentalizes, often unintentionally, the suffering and oppression of others for the self-preservation of the prophet's or the prophetic community's authenticity. Heroism of this sort can manifest itself in a prideful or despairing form. The usual use—surely a misuse—of the commonplace maxim, "Prophets are called to be faithful, not effective," slouches in the despairing direction. Rational criticism, which takes disciplined work beyond courage alone, aspires to the effective relief and release, to the effective healing and termination, of sufferings and oppression.

Third, Tillich argues that grace both fulfills prophetic criticism and overcomes it. Grace fulfills prophetic criticism by recognizing the necessity of prophetic and rational critique. For example, grace accomplishes its own purpose as prophetic critique notes the self-righteousness of a (false) rational criticism gone fanatical and the self-critique of a (false) prophetic criticism gone heroic. By stripping away fanatical and heroic self-righteousnesses, prophetic criticism prepares for a new form, the form of grace. As a herald of grace, prophetic criticism prepares for what is to come. Grace overcomes prophetic criticism by providing the form of grace to fanatics and heroes stripped of their self-righteousness by prophetic critique.

Fourth, Tillich suggests that the Protestant form of grace has most often appeared in the heroic personality and, further, that the distinctive Protestant form of grace might be the laicized heroic personality. Tillich rightly notes the limits and dangers of a laicized heroic personality, which resonates with my critique of an oracular prophetic imagination. Here we begin to see what the communicative imagination can contribute toward the Christian prophetic heritage. Can we imagine a laicized and communicative, and thereby nonheroic, prophetic personality?

Fifth, faced with the dangers of the laicized heroic personality, Tillich proposes the congregation as the Protestant form of grace. He suggests the congregation as the sociohistorical locus for the union of rational and prophetic criticism. By 1929, Tillich had not pursued this suggestion further. He does not investigate the everyday practices that could nurture the emergence of such congregations. He does not investigate the congregational habits that could dialectically unify rational and prophetic criticism within a sociohistorical situation. He does not probe more deeply the congregation as fecund soil for the prophetic imagination. Perhaps he did not, in 1929, have the conceptual tools to do so. As far as I can tell, Tillich left the prophetic imagination of the congregation in the lurch in 1929, but his suggestion is far too poignant to ignore. How might congregations become the sociohistorical locus for imagining and enacting rational and prophetic criticism for the sake of a more rational and just society? Further, how might congregations commit God's act of prophetic reasoning in public and thereby prepare for the eschatological arrival of the fullness of God's grace?[6] How does Habermas's communicative turn offer conceptual resources to develop Tillich's suggestion?

Habermas and the Communicative Turn of the Critical Theory of Society

First, Habermas confronts the extinguishing of the critical impulse that accompanied Horkheimer and Adorno's turn toward negative dialectics, with its totalistic and nihilistic critique of reason. Negative dialectics, which poignantly chronicles Nazism's descent into the demonic, also surrenders the field to demonic power. Habermas argues that Horkheimer's original hybrid approach to critical social theory, despite its difficulties and dead ends, was still a more fruitful way toward a more rational and just Western society. By unmasking the performative contradiction of negative dialectics, Habermas also points out the relativistic surrender to domination lurking in certain postmodern deconstructionist proposals, which are close cousins to negative dialectics. By celebrating the absence or the eclipse of reason, these proposals merely capitulate, even collaborate, with injustices accompanying the rise of certain neoconservatisms. Without normative resources—without reason—criticism burns out. Habermas's first aim, therefore, is to retrieve *reason, communicatively* reconstructed, in order to regenerate the normative bases of the critique of Western civilization. Moreover, a traditional philosophical—that is, epistemological—analysis of reason is not by itself sufficient to accomplish this retrieval and reconstruction. The retrieval and reconstruction of reason needs a multidisciplined, hybrid approach that attends diachronically to the interrelationship of social, economic, political, philosophical, cultural, and religious factors. These issues are crucial for prophetic reasoning and run parallel to Tillich's criticism of Marcuse and the need for prophetic depth.

Second, Habermas examines the dominant Western narrative of the rise of reason in order to retell the story. He emphasizes the simultaneous emergence of two kinds of reason, instrumental rationality and communicative rationality, and the prominence attained by the former to the detriment and repression of the latter. He investigates the dynamics of instrumental rationality—a subject/object form of reasoning—and why it came to dominate. In its dominance, instrumental rationality also takes shape as functional rationality, which underlies the great systems of Western life. Habermas's critique of functional rationality also depends on his sociological analysis of the emergence in the West of the great systems of the economy and politics, as we review shortly.

Third, Habermas critiques instrumental and functional rationalities by means of the theory of communicative rationality. Communicative rationality represents a paradigm shift for the contemporary assessment of reason. This theory seeks a form of reason with dynamics different from those of instrumental and functional rationality. Communicative rationality is an intersubjectively based form of reason rather than a form based within the atomistic subject, as are instrumental and functional forms. Two purposes guide Habermas's investigation of these different dynamics. First, within the dynamics of human communicative rationality, as human beings have evolved, lie the normative insights for humans' ongoing development. Second, the theory of communicative rationality provides the normative bases for Habermas's own epistemological and sociopolitical critiques of instrumental and functional rationalities. He knows that these sweeping and imposing claims demand cross-disciplinary and cross-cultural research, testing, and confirmation. According to Habermas's analysis, communicative reason does not eliminate the legitimate need for instrumental and functional forms of reason. Rather, communicative reason, when explicitly recognized, practiced, and socially located, can harness instrumental and functional rationalities for material production and political administration. The relationship between communicative reason and instrumental and functional rationalities can help disclose the dynamics of prophetic reason.

Fourth, Habermas takes up his demanding proposal by means of the linguistic turn in twentieth-century philosophy. Human language decisively fashions human existence. Humans purposely use language to reach mutual understanding. Habermas, however, moves beyond the standard linguistic turn by recognizing that this use of language happens not only in the face of misunderstanding, which philosophical hermeneutics studies, but also in the face of systematically distorted communication. For this reason, mutual understanding always involves, at least implicitly if not explicitly, making four different kinds of validity claims that aim for free and undistorted agreement. The quest for such agreement anticipates a communication community based on nothing but better arguments. Further, because every agreement is fallible, all remain subject to ongoing testing and the anticipation of future agreement by means of argumentation. The paradigm of a communicative form of reason, regarding claims to truth, takes its cue from the dynamics of argumentation.

Fifth, Habermas broadens the theory of communicative rationality into a theory of social action. Hence we have *communicative action.* The dynamics of communicative action take reason and action beyond instrumental and functional reason and instrumental and strategic action, which remain in bondage to the false notion of the solitary self, the atomistic subject, the autonomous individual. How might the Christian prophetic imagination, using these insights, move beyond the foreshortened horizon of the heroic, oracular prophet?

Sixth, Habermas initially situates communicative reason and action within the two-tiered sociological description of system and lifeworld. He describes the systems of the economy and the state functioning according to the media of money and administrative power. The lifeworld is the sphere mediated by the interpretation of tradition and finally by means of communicative reason and action. Habermas uses the dynamics of communicative action as a norm for assessing past and present interaction between system and lifeworld. In this way, the theory of communicative reason and action is a *critical theory of society.* That is, economy, state, and their respective media colonize the lifeworld, thwarting communicative reason and action. But despite the widespread colonization, communicative reason and action persistently give rise to new social movements at the intersections of system and lifeworld. Habermas thinks about ethnic movements for civil rights, women's movements, and ecological movements as examples. In light of these dynamics, prophetic reasoning needs to pay close attention to the colonization of the lifeworld.

Seventh, the proliferation of new social movements with their decolonizing proclivities stimulates Habermas in the 1990s to revise his sociological theory. He now situates communicative reason and action more within a three-tiered sociological portrait of lifeworld, civil society, and the systems of economy and state. Civil society is the public sphere that percolates with communicative rationality and action, which are rooted in the lifeworld. This new focus on civil society helps Habermas delineate three distinct models of democracy: the liberal, the republican, and the deliberative. The emergence of civil society functions as a political norm for preferring deliberative democracy over the other models of political democracy. Civil society, by communicatively generating, sustaining, strengthening, testing, and revising moral wisdom, action, and argumentation, helps prevent the colonizing tendencies of the economy and state, both controlled by money and administrative power. Civil society also helps promote the liberative use of money and power, which helps bring the economy and state under the normative accounting of communicative rationality and action. The central role of a communicative civil society can help us imagine how and where prophetic reasoning can influence contemporary Western contexts. We can also imagine how communicative prophetic imaginations might emerge again in Christian congregations.

Setting the Table

The Retrieval of Civil Society

It is no accident that Habermas revised his sociological theory in the early 1990s by attending more closely to civil society. Already before the 1989 collapse of the Soviet Union, Central and Eastern European dissidents were focusing on the renewal of civil society, even in the highly restricted versions in which it existed within the Soviet field of influence. These dissidents raised their fledgling democracies by nurturing churches, unions, neighborhoods, movements, and institutions.[7]

In the United States, we have lived with civil society for generations. In the decades since World War II, however, ordinary people in their everyday lives have, more often than not, come to take it for granted. The United States's entry into World War II necessitated the cooperation of the two great systems of modern life: the democratic state and the market economy. Our victories in World War II had much to do—not everything, but much—with the successful cooperation of these two systems under the leadership of Franklin D. Roosevelt. The collaborative success of the state and the market in the war effort progressively lured, even seduced, large numbers of ordinary Americans to fixate greatest attention and energies on the so-called real world of economy and state, impoverishing civil society as a valuable public space.

This growing fixation on the democratic state and/or the market economy draws on two of the rival Western heritages formulated over the last two centuries. Each of these intellectual heritages divulges a truth about the pursuit of the good life in the contemporary era, but each does so too one-sidedly.[8] The first is the neoclassical republican tradition proposed by Rousseau. This tradition highlights the moral agency of the *citizen,* which has been a key idea for democratic idealism. In the republican heritage, the constitutional *nation-state* is of highest worth, and nation-state citizenship is the telos that all moral agency must serve. The most telling criticism of this heritage does not concern constitutional democratic politics. I would argue vigorously that the democratic state is the best form for the modern era. Habermas's analyses of the republican and liberal models of the democratic state, however, help us see the deficiencies that even democracies can perpetuate. Moreover, though the democratic state touches ordinary living, it is not, paradoxically, the everyday life of many ordinary people. Ordinary people spend much of their time and energy earning a living.

Earning a living points to the second great Western heritage: the market capitalist tradition. This heritage spurns the republican fixation on the democratic state and focuses instead on the *economy* as the source of the good life; the *marketplace* is of highest worth. With market as the root metaphor, even the moral agency of economic production plays second fiddle to the consumptive path. The autonomous agency of personal, private choice satiates the spirit of the market heritage. Catering to the consumptive, choosing appetite are the entrepreneurs, who, perhaps more than consumers, are the ideal. In this *laissez-faire* system of classic liberalism, economic production, consumption, and entrepreneurship must remain liberated from the state. Even the democratic state must keep its hands off the economy.

The one-sidedness of the market capitalist heritage shows up in at least two ways. A growing number come to the marketplace with far too few resources to purchase or to produce the goods needed to participate effectively in our globalized economic life.[9] Many, and this number is also growing, come to the marketplace with enough or even an abundance of consumptive and entrepreneurial resources, but they do not find the good life. They find, instead, a meaningless, even a "heartless world." Many in this latter group search for a haven from the heartless world of the market-place, which is usually a cocoon like the nuclear family or the familially fashioned congregation. Ironically, the familially fashioned congregation provides a certain legitimacy for the normalcy of the heartless economy and state. Disturbingly, far too many find the private spaces to be equally, if not more, heartless than the marketplace or the democratic state. Such heart-lessness reveals that our private spheres remain fragile and cannot flourish without being rooted in and accountable to the broader moral networks and wisdoms that saturate civil society.[10] Furthermore, our private spaces too easily become colonized by the consumptive strategies of the market-place and by the administrative necessities of the democratic state.

Tragically, neither the republican nor the market heritages makes a theme of civil society, thus their one-sidedness. This fact, coupled with our half-century fixation on either the political or economic sphere, or even on some creative combination of the two, helps impoverish the moral poten-tiality and political significance of civil society. Finally, an impoverished civil society deprives us of a thriving deliberative democracy, which is essential for overcoming the colonizing effects of both money and admin-istrative power. An enriched civil society extends its deliberative-commu-nicative medium through the political public sphere to provide normative moorings for the state's administrative power. Civil society also extends its deliberative-communicative medium to the economy as a normative source for developing corporate responsibility, citizenship, and stakeholder ethos.

In our everyday lifeworld, we revel in our cultural heritages, coordinate our actions as groups according to mutually reached and recognized norms, and develop individual and social identities. These key features of the life-world—cultural embodiment, social integration, and socialization—have both a symbolic-metaphorical-linguistic and institutional dimensions. Civil society as a public space corresponds to the institutional dimension of our everyday lifeworld.[11] An enriched, communicative civil society imparts normative resources for a more emancipatory and just deliberative democ-racy and for a more responsible stakeholder economy, thereby weakening these great systems' colonizing effects. Surely nothing could be more inter-esting to the prophetic imagination? Further, an enriched, communicative civil society contributes directly to the more private spaces of lifeworld by providing a richer moral milieu than that possible when each individual, family, or heritage tries to stitch together its own moral code. Here, too, prophetic reason finds a vigorous vocation.

The Communicative Ethos of Civil Society

The descriptive account presented above assumes that civil society is satu-rated with communicative practices. That is not the case. Civil society as a sociological space is far more ambiguous. We need a normative account of civil society and, again, the communicative imagination will be the focus. Habermas's three models of democracy suggest that three different modes of civil society also exist. These modes impinge in different ways on civil society's contributions to the economy and state and to the lifeworld. Moreover, these forms have implications for the Christian prophetic imag-ination itself. We now examine the agonistic, liberal, and communicative modes of civil society. Historically, the first two forms have dominated the American imagination. Not surprisingly, these modes of civil society have also contributed to its current impoverishment as well as to a more heroic, oracular form of the Christian prophetic imagination.

The dominant practices of the agonistic ethos revolve around a "com-petitive struggle"—from the Greek *agōn*—among rival versions of personal and/or communal moral virtue. Within the public space of civil society, each rival communal tradition presents itself as a pure, self-sufficient, and cohesive totality of virtue. A tradition's moral virtuosity vies for preemi-nence over other communal traditions by displaying itself as publicly as possible. These traditions strive to gain the acclaim of the majority of citi-zens, who begin as passive onlookers, continue as active imitators, and fin-ish—at least an elite minority—as admired moral masters. Commonly, despite the differences among rival agonistic traditions, the internal social arrangements are alike in being hierarchically stratified. Commonplace among agonistic traditions is the root metaphor of the head mastering a body. This is the deep-seated Western *cephalous* tradition, which has vari-ous cross-cultural analogues.[12] These agonistic practices lead to the domi-nance of a single agenda of personal and communal virtue along with the diminution, assimilation, or outright elimination of rival communal tradi-tions. *Agonistic* refers, therefore, to the constellation of practices, forms, and attitudes just described. Furthermore, the agonistic model of civil soci-ety remains particularly susceptible to the technological temptations of the now-ubiquitous sound bite. Conventional clichés, simplistic stereotyping, and / or Manichaean scenarios exhaust the moral possibilities. Apocalyptic rhetoric often abounds. Communitarian heritages often promote an ago-nistic ethos, and so do Christian movements with sectarian slants or cata-comb aspirations.[13] Ironically, more conventional theocratic traditions, Christian and otherwise, also promote the agonistic mode of civil society.

One advantage of the agonistic model is that personal virtues for practical, face-to-face living are cultivated through the economy and politics, although systems are usually shielded from serious moral-prophetic consideration. While agonistic traditions often exude prophetic rhetoric across the political spectrum, they sunder prophetic insight from rational criticism, thereby retaining no aspiration to bring about serious social change. Here we have all the problems that Tillich perceived and that Habermas uncovered in his critique of negative dialectics. The social costs remain steep. In the modern history of Western societies, the agonistic ethos has corresponded and collaborated with the republican model of democracy. In the longer stretch of Western civilization, agonistic practices have collaborated with monarchic and aristocratic political arrangements. Agnostic practices have also saturated the more monarchic and aristocratic forms of ecclesial imagination and life. There is little surprise, then, that the domination of agonistic practices likewise constricts the prophetic imagination to the heroic, oracular personality or perhaps to the heroic, oracular tribe. But, must the Christian prophetic imagination be so confined?

The liberal ethos of civil society originated in order to squelch the moral elitist and totalizing consequences of the agonistic civil society. In the liberal ethos, moral discourse is subject to the conversational constraint of neutrality whenever a single moral tradition asserts that its moral conception of the good life is superior to others. This constraint of neutrality prohibits not only agonistic "trumping," but also "translating" moral disagreements into a supposedly neutral framework as well as "transcending" moral disagreements by imagining some hypothetical circumstance. Rather, according to the conversational constraint of neutrality, moral traditions must agree not to disagree in public about the things that are most important and, instead, must confine moral disagreements to private spheres. In this way liberalism embeds "repressive tolerance" in the center of its ethos.[14] Not only is disagreement privatized, but the very terrain of controverted subject matters is privatized.[15] Increasingly, liberal civil society accedes morally relevant issues to the private-sector economy, to lifestyle intimacy, or to a privatized conscience, religious or otherwise. Along the way, the liberal model also privatizes the congregation. By shuttling the potentially most significant moral issues to private spheres, the liberal model trumps other moral formulations. Paradoxically, the practices, forms, and attitudes of the liberal ethos contribute to the withering of civil society itself by reducing it to a buffer zone, ameliorating the market economy's colonization of the lifeworld. By suppressing the moral vigor of civil society, the liberal mode unwittingly leaves the functional rationality of the state too dominant and thereby too unaccountable to public communicative reasoning. Similarly, the liberal practice of conversational constraint consigns the prophetic imagination to private issues and, indeed, aspires to neutralize the publicness of prophetic reason.

Emerging historically in the midst of the two dominant models is the communicative mode of civil society. This innovative model takes its practices, procedures, and attitudes from the paradigm shift to communicative rationality and action. A communicative civil society shares certain features with the dominant models. Like the agonistic model and unlike the liberal model of neutrality, it welcomes and, indeed, accentuates questions of moral truth. Unlike the agonistic ethos, with its characteristic practices of elitist moral display and purist moral trumping, communicative civil society holds that claims to practical moral truth must be redeemed critically through participatory practices. Participatory procedures empower traditions and institutions to have a say in the formulation, stipulation, and adoption of moral norms, or, to use Habermas's terms, in justification and application. Boldly stated, communicative civil society "comes into existence whenever and wherever all affected by general social and political norms of action engage in a practical discourse, evaluating their validity."[16]

By elevating participatory and communicative aspects, the communicative model eschews the moral elitist, exhibitionist, and totalizing tendencies at the heart of the agonistic model without, however, succumbing to the liberal model of public moral neutrality. A communicative civil society anticipates, even extols, the capacity for creative moral possibilities and overlapping moral insights. This anticipation depends on thick moral traditions becoming socially embodied and mutually engaging according to communicative procedures and by means of communicative practices. A communicative civil society is not, however, naive. Communicative procedures and practices themselves anticipate the manipulations and systematic distortions that accompany the self-interested monologue of any single moral tradition, including moral traditions that include or highlight communicative procedures and practices.[17] Moreover, a communicative civil society recognizes the fallibilist character of every communicative moral consensus. By so doing, a communicative civil society always anticipates future argumentation regarding any temporal moral consensus. As Christian eschatological theology puts it, a "not yet" dimension remains in every "already" achieved moral consensus. This is a crucial aspect of the communicative ethos. Finally, the communicative model rescinds the overly rigid boundaries between the public and private and, instead, allows for overlapping terrains of public and private life.[18]

Along with identifying overlapping terrains, an emerging communicative civil society supplies durable goods, one might say, both to the economy and state and to the lifeworld. A prime moral claim of the communicative imagination is that the search for the common good ought to proceed as a common search for the good.[19] In this way, common searching—communicatively imagined—becomes a comprehensive moral good that serves the well-being of other moral goods.[20] Accentuating questions of moral truth has practical import. A communicative civil society frequently shares argumentatively tested moral wisdom with the everyday lifeworld. Further, a communicative civil society often spots the colonizing consequences of the instrumental and functional rationalities operating within the economy's medium of money and the state's medium of administrative power. In this way, a communicative civil society ascertains that the great systems also contribute causally to the heartlessness experienced within the everyday lifeworld. In all of these ways, the communicative turn in critical social theory offers insight for the prophetic imagination, thereby enlarging the scope and enriching the field of prophetic reason.

A communicative civil society also has moral import for the great systems. It is essential for a viable deliberative democracy, comparable in importance to the separation and interaction of governmental powers and branches, and generates a reasoned form of public opinion and will. A communicative civil society is also a key companion of an economic system that attends to more than the economic shareholders.[21] Finally, a communicative civil society is consequential for establishing, sustaining, and improving the intersections between a materially productive market economy and a deliberative democratic state. Along these intersections among the weightier contributions of a communicative civil society will be to focus questions regarding a just, sustainable, and ecologically productive market economy. These complex issues are crucial for overcoming the colonization of the lifeworld.

All these factors denote a future for the Christian prophetic imagination beyond the heroic, oracular personality or community. The emergence of a global civil society communicatively rooted contains implications far beyond what we can explore in this project. The possible mutual contributions between a global communicative civil society and a communicative prophetic imagination are staggering.

Communicatively Renewing the Prophetic Vocation of Missional Congregations as Public Companions

The return of North American congregations is noteworthy.[22] In an unprecedented way, specialists in many fields are taking up a disciplined study of congregations. But congregations are returning not merely as objects of study but, more importantly, as primal and productive centers of theological imagination. A period of lament, especially among mainline denominations, preceded this return. The lament grew out of a widespread malaise associated with empty pews, diminished coffers, loosening of denominational loyalties, confusion of clerical identity, doctrinal uncertainty, and all-out "worship wars," among other things. Precipitating this malaise was a mainline "Christendom habit" that had seduced great numbers of congregations into insular, sedentary, and ancillary modes of existence. For more than a quarter-century, vast numbers of congregations remained satisfied with the past glories and cultural hegemony that they thought they possessed in the 1950s. Many experts were composing dirges for these congregations, some with glee, others with regret.[23] The Christendom habit may still persist, but as a shadow of its former self, reduced no doubt to a therapeutics of personal refreshment and fulfillment.

A smaller but growing number of people are taking steps beyond Christendom's assumptions and habits.[24] In seeking a new missional ecclesiology in North America, they are confronting the poverty of missional imagination and contesting its inevitability. The Christian prophetic imagination must in a vital way suffuse this innovative missional aspiration. Without the Christian prophetic imagination, this critical retrieval of missional congregations and ecclesial reflection risks replicating the old insular and ancillary habits. I offer the communicative turn of critical social theory as a formidable companion for instilling prophetic imagination in missional congregations.

How can we develop missional congregations as public companions?[25] Developing Christian congregations in this way does not envision a return to Christendom, but an immersion in a pluralistic and ambiguous era of many cultures, religions, and irreligions. We can gain clarity about the metaphor "public companion" by situating it within H. Richard Niebuhr's now-classic typology of "Christ and culture," while also keeping in mind

Avery Dulles's helpful "models of the church."[26] Niebuhr maps five types of the relationship between Christ and culture, which can also be viewed fruitfully as a typology of church and culture.[27] At the polar extremes of the typology, he positions "Christ against culture"—imagine that on the left of the chart—and "Christ of culture"—imagine that on the right of the chart. The three remaining types—"Christ and culture in paradox" (the Lutheran type), "Christ transforming culture" (the Reformed type), and "Christ above culture" (the Roman Catholic type)—are positioned from left to right between the two poles. He describes these middle types as the churches of the center, the type on the left pole manifesting itself in the sectarian left wing of the Reformation, for instance, and the type on the right pole in the nineteenth-century liberal Protestant churches in Germany. The metaphor "public companions," especially when embodying insights and practices of the communicative imagination, resonates dissonantly with either the "Christ against culture" type or the "Christ of culture" type. Public companions in the communicative mode provide more prophetically critical engagement with culture than "Christ of culture" imagines and more proactive, prophetic healing than "Christ against culture" imagines. More resonance comes from the ecclesial heritages at the center of Niebuhr's typology. I have found it especially fruitful to gather and revise the fundamental claims made by the "Christ and culture in paradox" heritage.[28]

We can also gain more access to congregations as communicatively prophetic public companions by situating our metaphor within Dulles's "models of the church." He has five models. The first three are more Roman Catholic–oriented, and the latter two more Protestant-oriented. The Roman Catholic models are church as "institution," as "mystical communion," and as "sacrament." He offers these models as a way to chart the course that Roman Catholic ecclesiology has traveled leading up to and then flowing out of the Second Vatican Council (1962–1965). "Church as institution" summarizes ecclesial doctrine from the late Middle Ages and the Counter-Reformation, culminating in the First Vatican Council in the late nineteenth century. "Church as mystical communion" emerged in the first half of the twentieth century as a way to move beyond "church as institution." This new model was more communitarian and interpersonal than the first model and led to many of the developments of Vatican II, with its focus on church as the people of God and body of Christ. The third model, "church as sacrament," also emerged during the twentieth century and became an orienting doctrine of Vatican II. Because of the long heritage of

sacramental theology, this model provides, on the one hand, more disciplined theological reflection to the more metaphorical and biblical intu-
itions attached to "people of God" and "body of Christ." On the other
hand, "church as sacrament" also retrieves certain aspects of "institution,"
combining them with the communal features of "mystical communion."

The fourth and fifth models are "church as herald," which Lutherans
brought to prominence, and "church as servant," favored by Reformed
churches. The "church as herald" orients the church around gospel proclamation and toward enacting the gospel in and for the world. The "church
as servant" orients the church around divine service in the world. The
metaphor of public companionship aspires to embody both models and to
do so with the former providing the abundance necessary for the latter. The
metaphor also aspires to overcome the privatization that has colonized both
models. Various sociohistorical forces have often combined to reduce
"church as herald" to an abstract kerygmatic address, either objectifying
individual hearers or stimulating individual decisions of the will. These
forces also reduce "church as servant" to the habits of a service-sector economy, clinic, or family haven. These reductions have suppressed numerous
aspects of Christianity, surely including the prophetic dimension of the
Christian imagination. Here I offer the public-companion metaphor only
in reference to the prophetic imagination within the servant model.[29]

The Reformation developed the model of "servant" through its critical
theology of vocation.[30] Against the individualistic notion of vocation, the
concept includes the ways that everyone, knowingly or not, participates in
God's public, ongoing work to bring, nurture, and sustain temporal life. In
trusting the gospel of Jesus Christ, Christians acknowledge these places,
purposes, and institutions as God's creative work on behalf of their neighbors and nations, and themselves as God's companions. Likewise, congregations have a variety of vocations to bring God's creative agency to bear on
neighbors, neighborhoods, and nations. Building moral milieus to make
life in public communities possible commends itself as one such calling.
Civil society is the preferential, though not only, location for this congregational vocation of public companionship, and communicative moral
practice is the best ethos for prophetically nurturing the postmodern
milieu toward sustainable justice and freedom.[31]

Congregations participate in the moral life of the community in two
ways simultaneously, one practice more internal and the other more external. Internally, congregations have often assisted families and individuals in

moral formation, in particular of the young, and this will continue as a prime vocation. As congregations engage in moral formation, they can fall prey to seeing themselves as private Christian enclaves, alienated, isolated, and protected from the truth claims of other moral traditions. In our ever more pluralistic public environment, however, innumerable traditions ask congregations to offer justification, in the sense of ethical grounding, for the moral formation imparted. The communicative turn in critical social theory is a welcome companion as congregations take up the work of moral justification and application. Moreover, God regularly calls Christian congregations, through the prophetic imagination of the biblical heritage, to attend to the sufferings and oppressions of neighborhoods and nations. The normative depiction of deliberative democracy, obtained from critical social theory, helps congregations retrieve and embody the prophetic imagination within North American and global contexts. In all of these ways, congregations exist as meeting places of private and public life.[32]

In this role, congregations respond with integrity to their more external moral vocation as communicatively prophetic public companions. Today an increasing number and variety of institutions in civil society need public companions to join in encountering the moral meanings latent in contemporary life. This is a risky vocation, because Christian congregations do not have a monopoly on moral wisdom. As communicatively prophetic public companions, congregations become encumbered communities. They become encumbered with the moral predicaments of other institutions and with the colonizing influence of money and power. Christian congregations, however, are no stranger to an encumbered life, to a life of the cross. Herein lies the redemptive moment characterizing every vocation, when encumbered companionship puts a congregation's enclosed centrality to death.[33]

In summary, certain marks characterize the vocation of the communicatively prophetic, public companion. As prophetic public companions, missional congregations acknowledge a *conviction* that they participate in God's ongoing creative work. In a communicative civil society, these congregations exhibit a *compassionate commitment* to other institutions and their moral predicaments and to contesting the systemic colonization of the lifeworld. In these two senses, congregations as communicatively prophetic public companions are thoroughly connected, both to God and to the social and natural world. This vocational conviction and commitment yields a *critical* and *self-critical,* and thus fully *communicative,* practice of prophetic engagement. Finally, as communicatively prophetic public companions, congregations participate with other institutions of communicative civil society to *create, strengthen,* and *sustain* the moral fabrics that fashion a life-giving and life-accountable world.

Notes

Preface

1. Martin Luther King, Jr., *Why We Can't Wait* (New York: Signet Books, 1963) and Malcolm X, *The Autobiography of Malcolm X*, with the assistance of Alex Haley (New York: Grove Press, 1965).

2. King, ibid., 110.

3. Walter Brueggemann, as far as I am aware, coined the poignant phrase "the prophetic imagination;" see Walter Brueggemann, *The Prophetic Imagination* (Philadelphia: Fortress Press, 1978). I assume that he was inspired by C. Wright Mills's influential book, *The Sociological Imagination* (New York: Oxford University Press, 1959). Mills argued that in the face of the rapid structural transformations of the times people needed a sociological imagination. For Mills's own thoughts on the traits of the sociological imagination and its usefulness see especially *op. cit.*, 5-24.

4. Sociologist Stephen Warner has made this observation and has offered some helpful analysis. See R. Stephen Warner, "The Place of the Congregation in the Contemporary American Religious Configuration, in *American Congregations*, Vol. 2, *New Perspectives in the Study of Congregations*, eds. James Wind & James Lewis (Chicago: University of Chicago Press, 1994), 59-63.

5. Robert Michael Franklin, "The Safest Place on Earth: The Culture of Black Congregations," in Wind & Lewis, 257-284; and also idem, "When God Says Stay, You Stay!" in *Center City Churches: The New Urban Frontier*, ed. Lyle Schaller (Nashville: Abingdon Press, 1993), 21-30.

6. Critical social theory as a "creation of the early thirties [and] . . . a discovery of the late sixties" is Paul Connerton's poignant phrase; see Paul Connerton, "Introduction," in *Critical Sociology: Selected Readings*, ed. Paul Connerton (New York: Penguin Books, 1978), 12.

1. Horkheimer: The Idea of Critical Social Theory

1. The translators of Horkheimer's early studies recognized in the title of their volume the hybrid characteristic of his social philosophy (Max Horkheimer, *Between Philosophy and Social Science: Selected Early Writings*, trans. G. Hunter, M. Kramer, and

J. Torpey [Cambridge, Mass.: MIT Press, 1995]; henceforth abbreviated as *BPSS*).
Horkheimer introduced this hybridity as he explored the "boundary between" philosophy and sociology in his inaugural lecture (*BPSS* 8). For two exhaustive accounts of the
early years of the institute and its members, see Martin Jay, *The Dialectical Imagination:
A History of the Frankfurt School and the Institute of Social Research, 1923–1950* (Boston:
Little, Brown, 1973), and Rolf Wiggershaus, *The Frankfurt School: Its History, Theories,
and Political Significance* (Cambridge, Mass.: MIT Press, 1994).

2. *BPSS* 13. Horkheimer attributes this insight to Hegel (*BPSS* 359).

3. Ibid., 1.

4. I am indebted to Alvin Gouldner's historical reconstruction of early positivism
(see *The Coming Crisis of Western Sociology* [New York: Basic Books, 1970], 61–108).
Gouldner was a student teaching assistant for Horkheimer's colleague Theodor Adorno
while Adorno was teaching at Columbia University in New York.

5. Max Horkheimer, "Traditional and Critical Theory," in *Critical Theory: Selected
Essays*, trans. M. O'Connell et al. (New York: Seabury Press, 1972), 188–243 (henceforth, TCT). The original appeared as "Traditionelle und kritische Theorie," *Zeitschrift
für Sozialforschung* 6, no. 2 (1937): 245–94.

6. TCT 242.

7. In a footnote, Martin Jay perceptively notes that the Frankfurt School used the
term *positivism* in "a loose way" to include a variety of intellectual currents, some of
which strenuously protested being called positivist (*Dialectical Imagination,* 47).

8. TCT 196.

9. TCT 232ff.; also *CT* 186.

10. *BPSS* 315.

11. Ibid., 314–15.

12. TCT 213; see also TCT 195, 205, and *BPSS* 28, 245.

13. *CT* 157.

14. Descartes did acknowledge a "third" substance—God—but he was reticent to
reflect upon knowing God.

15. *CT* 141.

16. Ibid., 155f.

17. *BPSS* 218.

18. *CT* 36.

19. Ibid., 35, 144–48; also *BPSS* 315–16.

20. *CT* 149, 142.

21. Ibid., 5.

22. Ibid., 151.

23. TCT 199.

24. *CT* 246.

25. *BPSS* 314.

26. Ibid., 317.

27. Ibid., 319.

28. Ibid., 330.

29. Cited in ibid., 318; see Niccolò Machiavelli, *The Prince and the Discourses* (New
York: Modern Library, 1940), 149.

30. *BPSS* 337, 330–35.
31. Ibid., 339; from Thomas Hobbes, *De Cive,* ed. Howard Warrender (London: Oxford University Press, 1983), 32 (preface).
32. *BPSS* 344.
33. Ibid., 345.
34. Ibid., 21.
35. *CT* 245.
36. In a poignant phrase, Richard Bernstein calls this "the Cartesian anxiety" (*Beyond Objectivism and Relativism: Science, Hermeneutics, and Praxis* [Philadelphia: University of Pennsylvania Press, 1983], 16).
37. *CT* 157–59; TCT 202.
38. Cited by Horkheimer (TCT 203) from Immanuel Kant's *Critique of Pure Reason,* B 181.
39. TCT 210.
40. *BPSS* 178–79.
41. Ibid., 20.
42. Ibid., 24.
43. Ibid., 21.
44. Ibid., 19.
45. Ibid., 27.
46. TCT 240; also see *BPSS* 2.
47. TCT 211.
48. Ibid., 200.
49. *BPSS* 362.
50. Ibid., 184.
51. Ibid., 185.
52. *CT* 32; also see TCT 233–43.
53. *CT* 25; also see *BPSS* 30–31, 37–38.
54. *CT* 26.
55. Ibid., 45–46. Throughout his life, Horkheimer sought to bring suffering into sharp focus as a social problem. This lay at the heart of his critical social theory. We can see this clearly by reading his notes from the early years (see Max Horkheimer, *Dawn and Decline: Notes, 1926–1931 and 1950–1969,* trans. M. Shaw [New York: Seabury Press, 1978]).
56. TCT 227.
57. *BPSS* 355.
58. Ibid., 129–49.
59. Ibid., 63, 75–76, 350–51, 360.
60. Ibid., 139.
61. Ibid., 47.
62. TCT 229–32; also *BPSS* 51, 190ff.
63. TCT 213.
64. See David Held, *Introduction to Critical Theory: Horkheimer to Habermas* (Berkeley: University of California Press, 1980), 354–64.
65. TCT 219; also see 221–24, 229–30.
66. Ibid., 232.
67. Ibid., 233.

68. Ibid., 234.

69. Ibid., 238.

70. Ibid.

71. *BPSS* 388.

2. Tillich: Christian Engagement with Critical Social Theory

1. See Rolf Wiggershaus, *The Frankfurt School: Its History, Theories, and Political Significance* (Cambridge, Mass.: MIT Press, 1994), 37, 91–95.

2. Martin Jay, *The Dialectical Imagination: A History of the Frankfurt School and the Institute of Social Research, 1923–1950* (Boston: Little, Brown, 1973), 24. Tillich himself reports that his intellectual friendships during this period were with those discriminated against in Nazi Germany (see Hannah Tillich, *From Time to Time* [New York: Stein and Day, 1973], 141–56]).

3. Wiggershaus, *Frankfurt School,* 111.

4. The interpretive conflict was occasioned by the first translation into English of Tillich's *Socialist Decision,* trans. F. Sherman (1933; New York: Harper & Row, 1977). Among the social and political circumstances that stimulated this English translation after more than forty years was the emergence of Christian-Marxist dialogues in the United States, of Western Christian political theologies, and, of course, of Latin American liberation theologies. To varying degrees and in various ways, Marxist thought played a role in these developments.

5. Terrence O'Keeffe, "Paul Tillich and the Frankfurt School," in *Theonomy and Autonomy: Studies in Paul Tillich's Engagement with Modern Culture,* ed. John J. Carey (Macon, Ga.: Mercer University Press, 1984), 67.

6. Ronald Stone, "Tillich's Critical Use of Marx and Freud in the Social Context of the Frankfort [*sic*] School," *Union Seminary Quarterly Review* 33 (fall 1977): 3.

7. Ronald Stone, "Tillich: Radical Political Theologian," *Religion in Life* 46 (spring 1977): 44–53.

8. Stone, "Tillich's Critical Use of Marx and Freud," 3. Stone argued that the institute's model of social reality "is reflected in several areas of Tillich's thought" (4). Stone enumerated five areas: critical distance, the significance of Marx and Freud, the place of utopian thinking, anti-Semitism, and economics. Consideration of these issues would take us beyond the scope of my study.

9. O'Keeffe, "Paul Tillich and the Frankfurt School," 67.

10. Jay, *Dialectical Imagination,* 31–37. Rudolf Siebert, among others, takes up Jay's comment and enlarges it by suggesting that critical social theory becomes a secular equivalent and, indeed, substitution for the second commandment in Moses' decalogue: thou shalt not make for thyself a graven image (Rudolf Siebert, *The Critical Theory of Religion: The Frankfurt School* [Berlin and New York: Mouton, 1985], 116). This command prohibits utterance of the sacred name and rests on the recognition that the messianic age has not arrived. We come back to this idea shortly. Horkheimer comments briefly on this subject in later periods of his life (see, for instance, a remark from 1966–69 in Max Horkheimer, *Dawn and Decline: Notes, 1926–1931 and 1950–1969,* trans. M. Shaw [New York: Seabury Press, 1978], 236–37).

11. See Alvin Gouldner's discussion of the interpretive conflict over "real" Marxism

(*The Two Marxisms: Contradictions and Anomalies in the Development of Theory* [New York: Seabury Press, 1980]).

12. O'Keeffe, "Paul Tillich and the Frankfurt School," 80.

13. Ibid.

14. O'Keeffe notes that the institute's own publications never addressed Tillich's work, nor did they address articles that appeared during the 1920s and early 1930s in the two journals that Tillich edited. Further, only once during these years did Tillich mention the work of the institute, and then in a superficial manner. Yet, as we see later, Tillich in 1941 did write in the exiled institute's own journal an important review of Herbert Marcuse's work.

15. These issues of Marxist theory, dealing with the "early" and "late" Marx, with the more Hegelian strand, and with a "Western" brand of Marxism, lie beyond the scope of this inquiry. For these and similar issues, see Gouldner, *Two Marxisms.*

16. O'Keeffe, "Paul Tillich and the Frankfurt School," 83.

17. Ibid., 84.

18. Ibid., 86.

19. Ibid., 87.

20. James Champion, "Tillich and the Frankfurt School: Parallels and Differences in Prophetic Criticism," *Soundings* 69 (winter 1986): 514. When Champion says "common movement," he means what is common in Tillich's *The Socialist Decision* (1933) and Horkheimer and Adorno's *Dialectic of Enlightenment* (1944). We consider the latter work in chapter 3. Still, in the following pages I indicate where Horkheimer and Adorno take critical social theory during the 1940s and why.

21. Jay, *Dialectical Imagination,* 262.

22. Champion, "Tillich and the Frankfurt School," 513–15.

23. See, for instance, Ernst Bloch, *Man on His Own: Essays in the Philosophy of Religion* (New York: Herder & Herder, 1970).

24. Champion, "Tillich and the Frankfurt School," 514. That Champion misses the weightier difference between Horkheimer/Adorno and Tillich is illustrated in another way. He notes that Horkheimer's and Adorno's hidden prophetic dimension "underlies their conventional allegiance to the radical Enlightenment tradition of critical reason and forms a common center of gravity in their work" (515). By "the radical Enlightenment tradition of critical reason," Champion has Nietzsche, and perhaps Schopenhauer, in mind. Tillich, however, sharply differentiated himself from Nietzsche's tradition of critical reason. See Tillich, "Nietzsche and the Bourgeois Spirit," *Journal of the History of Ideas* 6 (June 1945): 307–9.

25. Champion, "Tillich and the Frankfurt School," 516.

26. Paul Tillich, review of *Reason and Revolution: Hegel and the Rise of Revolution,* by Herbert Marcuse, *Studies in Philosophy and Social Science* 9 (1941): 476–78 (henceforth, RRR).

27. Ibid., 476.

28. I cannot explore this criticism within this study. The Frankfurt School often lumped pragmatism with positivism. I expect that Tillich's criticism was his way of rescuing the American pragmatist traditions from the garbage heap of positivism.

29. RRR 477.

30. Ibid., 478.

31. For Tillich's 1929 exposition of "self-transcending realism" or "belief-ful realism" in comparison with other types of realism, see *The Protestant Era,* trans. J. L. Adams (Chicago: University of Chicago Press, 1957), 66–82 (henceforth, *PE*).

32. RRR 478.

33. Paul Tillich, "Protestantism as a Critical and Creative Principle," in *Political Expectation* (New York: Harper & Row, 1971), henceforth cited as PCCP. This essay is not for the faint of heart. Tillich is highly nuanced and dialectical in his discussion of the theological options of the 1920s and their relationships to the history of German idealism. Readers also must deal with Tillich's neologisms. For the searching and diligent, the effort yields generous dividends.

34. In 1935, Tillich engaged Barth's dialectical theology more thoroughly in "What Is Wrong with the 'Dialectic' Theology?" in *Paul Tillich: Theologian of the Boundaries,* ed. M. K. Taylor (London: Collins, 1987), 104–16.

35. PCCP 14.

36. Ibid., 10.

37. Ibid., 10–11.

38. Ibid.

39. Ibid., 12.

40. Since the emergence of critical social theory, we hardly ever in present-day English employ the trope "status quo" in the simple descriptive way in which the Latin uses it, that is, as "the state of that which is." As a trope, "status quo" carries a more evaluative, even pejorative, meaning, though with a critically hopeful edge or attitude. The phrase now connotes that "'the way it is' is exactly as the powerful would like you to think it is, but *it does not have to be that way.*"

41. That others may have a "flight" reflex in the same or similar situations implies that such reflexes in humans are perhaps not so immediate as was once thought, due to early gender- and culture-scripting.

42. PCCP 12.

43. Ibid.

44. Ibid.

45. Ibid. By "the *conditioned* transcendent of spirit," Tillich likely means something close to cultural spirit or even plain culture (see Paul Tillich, *What Is Religion?* ed. L. J. Adams [New York: Harper & Row, 1969], 155–63).

46. PCCP 16.

47. Ibid., 12.

48. Ibid.

49. Tillich puts it provocatively: "[R]adically negative judgments . . . against self-sufficient autonomy has had a real justification both historically and in principle" (ibid., 13).

50. Ibid., 14.

51. Ibid., 12–13. Tillich's parenthetical reference to "crisis" is a double entendre, because dialectical theology was also called "crisis theology."

52. Ibid., 13.

53. Ibid., 13–14.

54. In chapter 3, we discover that Habermas offers a similar analysis of the fate of the critical impulse in the negative dialectics of Horkheimer and Adorno.

55. PCCP 14.

56. Ibid., 15.

57. Tillich asserts that "a glance at history, for example, the history of social criticism, confirms this statement with overwhelming force" (ibid., 14). He does not support this assertion with examples in this essay, much less with historical analysis. He merely footnotes the assertion, saying that it "has been sufficiently established" that Western social criticism depends on Old Testament prophetism. Does he perhaps have Ernst Troeltsch's *The Social Teaching of the Christian Churches* in mind?

58. PCCP 15.

59. Ibid.

60. For Tillich's general indebtedness to the Lutheran legacy, see *On the Boundary: An Autobiographical Sketch* (New York: Charles Scribner's Sons, 1966), 74–81.

61. PCCP 15.

62. Ibid., 16.

63. Ibid., 17.

64. Ibid., 18. Also see Tillich's reflections on Protestantism as protest and form in *The Religious Situation,* trans. H. R. Niebuhr (New York: Meridian Books, 1932), 191–207.

65. In another exploration, Tillich says:

> The peril of Protestantism lay in the fact that it was a protest and that it did not achieve an adequate realization. No church can be founded on a protest, yet Protestantism became a church. Consequently, it needed to adopt positive elements out of tradition, but in such a way that they would not take the edge off the force of the protest; therefore it limited them and crowded them into the background to the point of neglect. As a result the protest lost its ultimate meaning and became a doctrine alongside other doctrines. This inner dilemma of Protestantism lies in this, that it must protest against every religious or cultural realization which seeks to be intrinsically valid, but that it needs such realization if it is to be able to make its protest in any meaningful way.
>
> All the separate problems of Protestantism in the present situation grow out of this inner contradiction which constitutes at the same time its greatness and its tragedy. (*The Religious Situation*, 192–93)

66. PCCP 18.

67. Ibid. He does not explain why the presupposition of prophetic criticism would not be prophetic form; he has already argued that the presupposition of rational criticism is rational form. He never discusses why he departs from a strict parallelism. Why does prophetic criticism immediately presuppose "form of grace" and not "prophetic form," as one might think?

68. Ibid., 22.

69. Ibid., 23.

70. Ibid., 24.

71. Ibid.

72. Ibid., 25.

73. Ibid., 26.

74. In a footnote, Tillich remarks that he and Barth have "eschatological thinking" in common, though Barth "overlooks" the significance of anticipation (ibid., 26).

75. Ibid. Already in his famous 1922 article, "Kairos," Tillich had argued quite similarly. "Everything can be a vessel of the unconditional, but nothing can be unconditioned itself" (*PE* 47).

76. PCCP 27.

77. Ibid., 28. In 1922, Tillich used the term "theonomous culture" to describe this phenomenon (*PE* 44, 220).

78. PCCP 27. It is noteworthy, given the discussion in our day about the nature of public, Christian claims to truth and whether and in what way these claims might be subject to criteria that do not proceed directly from the Christian narrative, that Tillich argues that the form of grace expressed as religious culture is subject to rational criticism and not only to prophetic criticism. Still, Tillich is always keenly attentive to the dynamic relationship between rational and prophetic criticisms.

79. Ibid.

80. Ibid., 28.

81. Ibid., 27.

82. Ibid., 28.

83. Ibid., 29.

84. Ibid., 30.

85. Ibid., 31.

86. Ibid. I think that Tillich abandoned this "vocation" form of grace far too prematurely. What if he had turned not so much to the laicizing of monastic, interior disciplines but rather to laicized worldly vocation? Could his imagination go no further than an interior mode of piety?

87. Ibid.

88. Ibid., 32.

89. Ibid., 33.

90. Ibid., 33, 34.

91. See Tillich's comment on his use of the terms *culture* and *civilization* in *PE* 219.

92. PCCP 34.

93. Ibid., 36.

94. Ibid., 37.

95. Ibid., 38. He introduces *kairos* abruptly and, in this essay, does not develop it sufficiently to relate it to the relationship between rational and prophetic criticism. For his earlier (1922) exposition, see *PE* 32–51.

96. PCCP 38.

97. Ibid., 35.

98. Dennis McCann, "Tillich's Religious Socialism: 'Creative Synthesis' or Personal Statement?" in *The Thought of Paul Tillich,* ed. J. L. Adams, W. Pauck, and R. Shinn (San Francisco: Harper & Row, 1985), 81–101. For McCann's full comparative treatment of liberation theology and Christian realism, see *Christian Realism and Liberation Theology: Practical Theologies in Creative Conflict* (Maryknoll, N.Y.: Orbis Books, 1981).

99. McCann, "Tillich's Religious Socialism," 96–97.

100. Ibid., 100–101.

101. Ibid., 97.

102. McCann has investigated Habermas's earlier work at length ("Habermas and the Theologians," *Religious Studies Review* 7 [1981]: 14–21) and has enlisted it constructively in his own proposals (see Dennis McCann and Charles Strain, *Polity and Praxis: A Program for American Practical Theology* [Minneapolis: Winston, 1985], and Dennis McCann, *New Experiment in Democracy: The Challenge for American Catholicism* [Kansas City, Mo.: Sheed & Ward, 1987]).

3. Criticism: The Transformation of Critique

1. Theodor Adorno et al., *The Positivist Dispute in German Sociology,* trans. G. Adey and D. Frisby (London: Heinemann, 1976). Rolf Wiggershaus offers a detailed discussion of this dispute in *The Frankfurt School: Its History, Theories, and Political Significance,* trans. M. Robertson (Cambridge, Mass.: MIT Press, 1994), 566–82. Also see Robert Holub's discussion of the positivist dispute in *Jürgen Habermas: Critic in the Public Sphere* (London: Routledge, 1991), 20–48. The strength of Holub's book lies in taking up Habermas's debates—in addition to the positivist dispute—with Hans-Georg Gadamer's hermeneutics, with the 1960s' student left movement, with Niklas Luhmann's systems theory, with Jean-François Lyotard's postmodernism, and with the Holocaust revisionist historians.

2. Jürgen Habermas, *The Philosophical Discourse of Modernity,* trans. F. Lawrence (Cambridge, Mass.: MIT Press, 1987), 120 (henceforth *PDM*).

3. Jürgen Habermas, *The Theory of Communicative Action,* vol. 1: *Reason and the Rationalization of Society* (Boston: Beacon Press, 1984), 366 (henceforth *TCA* 1). For Habermas's own revealing account of the development of his philosophical thinking, see *Autonomy and Solidarity: Interviews with Jürgen Habermas,* ed. P. Dews, rev. ed. (London: Verso, 1992), 147–85.

4. Max Horkheimer and Theodor Adorno, *Dialectic of Enlightenment,* trans. J. Cumming (New York: Continuum, 1995), xi (henceforth *DE*); cited by Habermas in *TCA* 1 386, 454 n. 70; and in *PDM* 118.

5. Max Horkheimer, *Eclipse of Reason* (New York: Seabury Press, 1974), 182 (henceforth *ER*).

6. See Alvin Gouldner's account of Marx's search for an emancipatory agent in *Against Fragmentation: The Origins of Marxism and the Sociology of Intellectuals* (New York: Oxford University Press, 1985), 3–27.

7. *ER* v.

8. Ibid., v–vi.

9. For Horkheimer's indebtedness to Weber, see the lengthy footnote in *ER* 6. Horkheimer seems to reflect the "loss of meaning" that Weber analyzed in "Religious Rejections of the World and Their Directions," in *From Max Weber: Essays in Sociology,* translated, edited, and with an introduction by H. H. Gerth and C. W. Mills (New York: Galaxy Book, 1958), 350–57. Gerth and Mills's introduction is a good starting point for understanding Weber and his general influence.

10. For an extensive analysis of Weber and his influence on critical social theory,

see *TCA* 1 143–271, 345–65. Habermas also notes that, with regard to formal and substantive types of reason, Weber's "own formulations are not very clear" (*TCA* 1 170).

11. See *TCA* 1 168–78.

12. *ER* 6.

13. Ibid., 5.

14. Ibid., 4–5.

15. Ibid., v.

16. The phrase "critique of instrumental reason" was the original German title of the lectures eventually published as *Eclipse of Reason.*

17. *ER* 32.

18. Ibid., 16.

19. Ibid., 17–18.

20. Ibid., 6.

21. Ibid., 7–8.

22. Ibid., 5, 31, 8, 24, 21.

23. *ER* 22. For an exposition of Weber's understanding of the "disenchantment of the world," a phrase borrowed from Friedrich Schiller, see *TCA* 1 243–48.

24. *ER* 36–40.

25. Max Weber, *The Protestant Ethic and the Spirit of Capitalism,* trans. T. Parsons (New York: Charles Scribner's Sons, 1958), 181.

26. *ER* 98.

27. Ibid., 93. Horkheimer's colleague, Theodor Adorno, in *Negative Dialectics* (New York: Seabury Press, 1973), called this "self-assertion gone wild." That is, the dominating self-assertion of humans over the natural world has become the self-assertive domination over humanness.

28. *ER* 40.

29. Ibid., 108.

30. Ibid., 93.

31. Ibid., 128.

32. Jürgen Habermas, "The Entwinement of Myth and Enlightenment: Re-reading *Dialectic of Enlightenment,*" *New German Critique* 26 (spring/summer 1982): 22 (henceforth EME); this important essay, in a different translation, is included in *The Philosophical Discourse of Modernity.*

33. *ER* 176.

34. *TCA* 1 382; the italics are mine, and I use them because Habermas explores these themes in depth. Habermas, following the quotation, references *ER* 177.

35. EME 22; also *PDM* 119. "The critique of instrumental reason conceptualized as negative dialectics renounces its theoretical claim while operating with the means of theory" (*TCA* 1 387).

36. Jürgen Habermas, "Remarks on the Development of Horkheimer's Work," in *On Max Horkheimer: New Perspectives,* ed. S. Benhabib, W. Bonss, and J. McCole (Cambridge, Mass.: MIT Press, 1993), 49–65.

37. *PDM* 56. For an earlier criticism of Nietzsche, see Jürgen Habermas, *Knowledge and Human Interests,* trans. J. Shapiro (Boston: Beacon Press, 1971), 290–300.

38. See *DE* 119; see *PDM* 110–12.

39. *PDM* 123; see Friedrich Nietzsche, *On the Genealogy of Morals,* trans. W. Kaufmann and R. Hollingdale (New York: Vintage Books, 1967), 153.

40. *PDM* 123; here Habermas references Friedrich Nietzsche, *Beyond Good and Evil: Prelude to a Philosophy of the Future,* trans. W. Kaufmann (New York: Vintage Books, 1966), 341.

41. *PDM* 123.

42. Ibid., 124.

43. Ibid., 126; Habermas refers to Nietzsche, *On the Genealogy of Morals,* 27–28, 112.

44. For Habermas's interpretation of Adorno's development from *Negative Dialectics* (trans. E. Ashton [New York: Seabury Press, 1973]) to *Aesthetic Theory* (trans. C. Lenhardt [London: Routledge & Kegan Paul, 1984]), see *PDM* 68 as well as Jürgen Habermas, "Theodor Adorno: The Primal History of Subjectivity—Self-Assertion Gone Wild," in *Philosophical-Political Profiles,* trans. F. Lawrence (Cambridge, Mass.: MIT Press, 1985), 101–11.

45. *TCA* 1 382.

46. *PDM* 68.

47. Ibid., 129.

48. Ibid., 5, 4.

49. Ibid.,128; see also 112, 113, 121, 129. For instance, Habermas argues that Marcuse rejected such resignation to the totalization of instrumental reason and thereby looked for a way out of Horkheimer's conundrum (see Jürgen Habermas, "Psychic Thermidor and the Rebirth of Rebellious Subjectivity," in *Habermas and Modernity,* ed. R. Bernstein [Cambridge, Mass.: MIT Press, 1985], 67–77).

50. *PDM* 129, 112–13, 121, 114, 129.

51. *TCA* 1 xli.

4. Theory: The Theory of Communicative Reason and Action

1. Jürgen Habermas, *The Theory of Communicative Action,* vol. 1: *Reason and the Rationalization of Society,* trans. T. McCarthy (Boston: Beacon Press, 1984), 390 (henceforth *TCA* 1).

2. Seyla Benhabib raises this poignant question in *Critique, Norm, and Utopia: A Study of the Foundations of Critical Theory* (New York: Columbia University Press, 1986), 221.

3. Jürgen Habermas, *The Philosophical Discourse of Modernity: Twelve Lectures,* trans. F. Lawrence (Cambridge, Mass.: MIT Press, 1987), 68 (henceforth *PDM*). Habermas cites this same passage from Theodor Adorno (*Negative Dialektik* [Frankfurt, 1973], 192) on at least two other occasions: in *TCA* 1 390 and in his essay from 1969, "Theodor Adorno: The Primal History of Subjectivity—Self-Affirmation Gone Wild," in *Philosophical-Political Profiles,* trans. F. Lawrence (Cambridge, Mass.: MIT Press, 1985), 108–9 (volume henceforth cited as *PPP*).

4. *PPP* 109.

5. Jürgen Habermas, *Autonomy and Solidarity: Interviews with Jürgen Habermas,* ed. P. Dews, rev. ed. (London: Verso, 1992), 193–94 (henceforth *AS*).

6. *TCA* 1 387, 392.

7. *PDM* 63.

8. *TCA* 1 387; see also Jürgen Habermas, *Postmetaphysical Thinking: Philosophical Essays,* trans. W. Hohengarten (Cambridge, Mass.: MIT Press, 1992), 58–59 (henceforth *PT*).

9. *PDM* 77. Also see Jürgen Habermas, *Theory and Practice,* trans. J. Viertel (Boston: Beacon Press, 1973), 156 (henceforth *TP*).

10. *PDM* 63–64.

11. Ibid., 295.

12. Ibid. Habermas includes among those who did not take alternative paths the young Hegel, the young Marx, the Martin Heidegger of *Being and Time,* and Jacques Derrida in his discussion with Husserl.

13. *PDM* 74.

14. Georg Hegel, *Phenomenology of Spirit,* trans. A. Miller (Oxford: Oxford University Press, 1977).

15. *TP* 142.

16. Ibid., 169.

17. See Jürgen Habermas, *Knowledge and Human Interests,* trans. J. Shapiro (Boston: Beacon Press, 1971), 5–63 (henceforth *KHI*).

18. Ludwig Wittgenstein, *Tractatus Logico-Philosophicus* (New York: Hardcourt, Brace, 1947).

19. Jürgen Habermas, *On the Logic of the Social Sciences,* trans. S. Weber Nicholsen and J. Stark (Cambridge, Mass.: MIT Press, 1991), 119 (henceforth *OLSS*).

20. See Ludwig Wittgenstein, *Philosophical Investigations,* trans. G. Anscombe, 3rd ed. (New York: Macmillan, 1962), 23; see *OLSS* 120–23.

21. Wittgenstein, *Philosophical Investigations,* 7; "We can also think of the whole process of using words . . . as one of those games by means of which children learn their native language. I will call these games 'language games.' . . ." Wittgenstein's insights have had a profound effect on numerous contemporary Christian theologians; among the most influential is George Lindbeck (see *The Nature of Doctrine: Religion and Theology in a Postliberal Age* [Philadelphia: Westminster Press, 1984]).

22. See *OLSS* 125, 130; *PT* 62.

23. *PT* 62.

24. Ibid., 63.

25. *OLSS* 147.

26. Ibid., 148–49.

27. Ibid., 144; Hans-Georg Gadamer, *Truth and Method* (New York: Crossroad, 1975), 363. Gadamer's insights have made a very important contribution to contemporary Christian theology. We can see this in many theologians; among the most significant is David Tracy (*The Analogical Imagination: Christian Theology and the Culture of Pluralism* [New York: Crossroad, 1981]). Because of this contribution, we follow closely Habermas's own thoughts about Gadamer.

28. *OLSS* 144.

29. Ibid.

30. Ibid., 146–47. Due to space limitations, I offer only a streamlined summary of the translation's most salient features.

31. Ibid., 145.

32. Ibid., 146.

33. Ibid.

34. Gadamer, *Truth and Method*, 217, 269.

35. *OLSS* 147–48.

36. Gadamer, *Truth and Method*, 273.

37. Ibid., 245.

38. Ibid., 239–40.

39. Ibid., 241–42.

40. Ibid., 267f.

41. *OLSS* 155.

42. Ibid., 154; Gadamer, *Truth and Method*, 263–64.

43. *OLSS* 152.

44. Ibid., 152; Gadamer, *Truth and Method*, 261.

45. *OLSS* 162, 164.

46. Ibid., 162.

47. Ibid., 163.

48. Ibid., 163–64.

49. Jürgen Habermas, "On Hermeneutics' Claim to Universality," in *The Hermeneutic Reader: Texts of the German Tradition from the Enlightenment to the Present,* ed. K. Mueller-Vollmer (New York: Continuum, 1997), 313 (article henceforth cited as OHCU).

50. Ibid., 314–16.

51. Gadamer, *Truth and Method,* 269; *OLSS* 169.

52. OHCU 314; taken from Albrecht Wellmer, *Critical Theory of Society,* trans. J. Cumming (New York: Continuum, 1971), 47. Among the many places where Habermas makes the same point in reference to Gadamer's hermeneutics, see *TP* 11–12.

53. *PT* 139; *PDM* 322.

54. Jürgen Habermas, "On Systematically Distorted Communication," *Inquiry* 13 (1970): 206.

55. *OLSS* 170.

56. OHCU 315. For Habermas's notion of *anticipation* and its significance, see Jürgen Habermas, *Justification and Application: Remarks on Discourse Ethics,* trans. C. Cronin (Cambridge, Mass.: MIT Press, 1993), 30–32 (henceforth *JA*). Eschatological theologian Wolfhart Pannenberg argues vigorously for the close connection between the anticipatory structure of reason and Christian theology (see *Theology and the Philosophy of Science* [Philadelphia: Westminster Press, 1976], 97–103, 185–90, 310–11; and *Systematic Theology,* vol. 1 [Grand Rapids: Eerdmans, 1991], 54–61, 245–49).

57. Habermas gives a simplified explanation of "reconstructive sciences" in OHCU 298. He offers more thoroughly argued renditions of his reconstructive approach in *TP* 22–24; in *Communication and the Evolution of Society,* trans. T. McCarthy (Boston: Beacon Press, 1979), 8–20 (henceforth *CES*); and in *Moral Consciousness and Communicative Action,* trans. C. Lenhardt and S. Weber Nicholsen (Cambridge, Mass.: MIT Press, 1990), 21–42 (henceforth *MCCA*).

58. *MCCA* 197.

59. For Habermas's discussion of the relationship between communicative transcendence and immanence, see *MCCA* 89–102 and *PDM* 297–98, 322–26.

60. Jürgen Habermas, "Concluding Remarks," in *Habermas and the Public Sphere,* ed. C. Calhoun (Cambridge, Mass.: MIT Press, 1992), 477.

61. Habermas calls his own comprehensive theory of speech-acts "universal pragmatics," because it analyzes the core, universal features of the use or pragmatics of speech. The pragmatic dimension of speech, compared for instance to the semantic dimension, focuses on speech as the communication between speech partners. For Habermas's line of inquiry leading up to his appropriation of Austin and Searle, see *TCA* 1 274ff. In volume 2 of *TCA*, Habermas works extensively with George Herbert Mead, whom Habermas credits with initiating the paradigm shift to communicative reason as the basis of social life. Due to the limited scope of this study, we sketch only the results of Habermas's appropriation of the paradigm shift and not his extensive investigation of Mead's formulations.

62. *CES* 26–33 and *TCA* 1 95, 274–75.

63. *CES* 34–50. The title of Austin's book is *How to Do Things with Words* (Cambridge: Harvard University Press, 1962). John Searle's book is *Speech Acts: An Essay in the Philosophy of Language* (Cambridge: Cambridge University Press, 1969).

64. *CES* 54.

65. Ibid., 53.

66. Ibid. We can see here why reconstruction of implicit know-how is crucial. Austin took our implicit know-how regarding "doing things with words" and made it into "know-that," or "how to," as he puts it.

67. Ibid., 29–30.

68. Ibid., 50–59; *TCA* 1 276–78.

69. *CES* 26–31.

70. Ibid., 53.

71. *TCA* 308.

72. *CES* 59.

73. Ibid., 3.

74. *TCA* 1 321.

75. *CES* 3.

76. *TCA* 1 335. This research leads Habermas to give systematic attention to the notion of *lifeworld,* which we examine in chapter 5.

77. Ibid., 336.

78. Ibid., 332; *CES* 208–10.

79. *CES* 4.

80. Ibid., 64. Habermas offers a helpful clarification about the relationship of reason, argumentation, and communicative action in "A Reply," in *Communicative Action: Essays on Jürgen Habermas's "The Theory of Communicative Action,"* ed. A. Honneth and H. Joas (Cambridge, Mass.: MIT Press, 1991), 223.

81. *TCA* 1 317.

82. Ibid., 17–18.

83. *CES* 63–64.

84. *JA* 156–65; see also *TCA* 1 25–42 and *MCCA* 32, 86–92. Readers with a serious philosophical bent will find these passages interesting, as Habermas discusses in what ways he is or is not either Kantian or Hegelian in these matters.

85. Habermas develops the framework for communicative ethics in *MCCA.* For the

key critical discussion of communicative ethics, see *The Communicative Ethics Controversy*, ed. S. Benhabib and F. Dallmayr (Cambridge, Mass.: MIT Press, 1990). Also see William Rehg, *Insight and Solidarity: A Study in the Discourse Ethics of Jürgen Habermas* (Berkeley: University of California Press, 1994).

86. *TCA* 1 24–26. Habermas often uses the phrase "the unforced force of the better argument" (see *MCCA* 87–89; also see *JA* 163).

87. Habermas, "Concluding Remarks," 467. Alvin Gouldner has stated this beautifully in reference to reason (see *The Dialectic of Ideology and Technology: The Origins, Grammar, and Future of Ideology* [New York: Oxford University Press, 1976], 216).

> "Reasonable" men [*sic*] require that they give, that they be given, and that they heed reasons; although what will be taken to be a convincing reason varies widely in different times and places. The giving of reasons is a way of securing consent to a given allocation of gratifications that is functionally alternative to the exertion of domination, where others are compelled to accept things for fear of violence. To give reasons is to communicate something about the self: that one is the kind of person who is loathe to use force and violence. To give reasons is subliminally to assure the other that violence against him is not imminent. To give reasons presents oneself as a responsible agent acting on his own account and accepting the other as such, rather than, say, simply as an agent susceptible to control by magic or by gods to whom one can appeal. To give reasons implies also that the other could withhold his cooperation (or forbearance) and that he cannot be coerced into this.

88. *JA* 32; *MCCA* 93. Habermas takes up the critical objections to his principle in *JA* 57–60.

89. I am indebted to Robert Bertram for this poignant way of stating the communicative-ethics maxim. What I have learned from him goes far beyond this maxim. He introduced me to Habermas's work and encouraged and helped me to develop its potential for Christian theology.

90. *JA* 38–39.

91. Ibid., 163.

92. Helmut Peukert in particular has pressed Habermas on the notion of an unlimited communicative community (see *Science, Action, and Fundamental Theology: Toward a Theology of Communicative Action*, trans. J. Bohman [Cambridge, Mass.: MIT Press, 1984]). Peukert argues that the Christian claim about the resurrection of Jesus is a better warrant for an unlimited communicative community than Habermas's more utopian idea. Also see the important collection of essays in D. Browning and F. Fiorenza, eds., *Habermas, Modernity, and Public Theology* (New York: Crossroad, 1992), which includes a response by Habermas. For another critical appraisal of why Habermas's communicative imagination needs a theological-religious referent, see Franklin Gamwell, *Democracy on Purpose: Justice and the Reality of God* (Washington, D.C.: Georgetown University Press, 2000), 1–9, 239–55.

93. *JA* 1–8. In everyday English in the United States, people use the words *ethical* and *moral* quite interchangeably. Habermas is using these words as specific technical

categories, as philosophical ethics most often uses them. Sometimes ethics uses the parallel of the purposive, the good, and the just, and Habermas does also. Again, however, these categories reflect technical usage and not ordinary usage. By distinguishing the tasks of practical reason and conceptualizing them the way he does, Habermas clarifies the critical relationship between communicative ethics and more neo-Aristotelian and Hegelian conceptualizations, on the one hand, and more Kantian and liberal conceptualizations, on the other. Among the many places that Habermas discusses these issues, see *AS* 223–61.

94. *JA* 8–17. We can only begin to sketch a few of the many features of Habermas's communicative ethics. For a look at other features of communicative ethics, see my "Human Nature and Communicative Ethics," in *Investigating the Biological Foundations of Human Morality,* ed. J. Hurd, Symposium Series 37 (Lewiston, N.Y.: Edwin Mellen Press, 1996), 195–208; this essay also appeared in *Dialog* 33 (fall 1994): 280–87.

95. In my reading, Habermas seems unclear about whether and how discourses of justification overlap the tasks of ethical prudence and moral right (see *JA* 6–14). In his "Translator's Introduction," Ciaran Cronin registers the complexity of this issue but, to my mind, does not provide clear guidance about Habermas's formulation or the adequacy of his formulation (see *JA* xxvi–xxvii).

96. *JA* 13.

97. Ibid., 176.

98. Habermas's participations in practical reasoning in Germany are inaccessible to English-speaking audiences, since only some have been translated. See, for instance, Jürgen Habermas, *A Berlin Republic: Writings on Germany,* trans. S. Rendall (Lincoln: University of Nebraska Press, 1997); and idem, *The New Conservatism: Cultural Criticism and the Historians' Debate,* ed. S. Weber Nicholsen (Cambridge, Mass.: MIT Press, 1989). From an earlier time, see Jürgen Habermas, *Toward a Rational Society: Student Protest, Science, and Politics,* trans. J. Shapiro (Boston: Beacon Press, 1970).

99. *TCA* 1 94.

100. Ibid., 100.

5. Society: Civil Society and Deliberative Democracy

1. Habermas briefly discusses (in 1989) the difference between real reform and romanticist revolution. See "Concluding Remarks," in *Habermas and the Public Sphere,* ed. C. Calhoun (Cambridge, Mass.: MIT Press, 1992), 469–75. In 1992, he notes that democratic revolution "is not a possession we simply accept as our fortunate inheritance from the past. Rather it is a project we must carry forward in the consciousness of a revolution both permanent and quotidian" (see *Between Facts and Norms: Contributions to a Discourse Theory of Law and Democracy,* trans. W. Rehg [Cambridge, Mass.: MIT Press, 1996], 470 [henceforth *BFN*]; "Concluding Remarks," 463–72).

2. *BFN* 330.

3. Jürgen Habermas, *The Structural Transformation of the Public Sphere: An Inquiry into a Category of Bourgeois Society,* trans. T. Burger and F. Lawrence (Cambridge, Mass.: MIT Press, 1989), 5–12 (henceforth *STPS*).

4. Ibid., 20. Alvin Gouldner's extensive historical analysis of the press is a helpful companion to Habermas's work (see *The Dialectic of Ideology and Technology: The Origins, Grammar, and Future of Ideology* [New York: Oxford University Press, 1976], 91–166).

5. *STPS* 23, 26.

6. Ibid., 24, 25, 25–26.

7. Ibid., 27.

8. Ibid., 181.

9. Ibid., 184, 193.

10. Ibid., 195.

11. See Jürgen Habermas, "Further Reflections on the Public Sphere," in Calhoun, *Habermas and the Public Sphere,* 435–41 (article henceforth cited as FRPS).

12. Jürgen Habermas, *Legitimation Crisis,* trans. T. McCarthy (Boston: Beacon Press, 1975), 1–7.

13. FRPS 425–30, 442–43.

14. Jürgen Habermas, *The New Conservatism: Cultural Criticism and the Historians' Debate,* trans. S. Weber Nicholsen (Cambridge, Mass.: MIT Press, 1989), 62–69 (henceforth *NC*); *BFN* 171, 299, 330, 371–74.

15. Jürgen Habermas, *The Theory of Communicative Action,* vol. 2: *Lifeworld and System,* trans. T. McCarthy (Boston: Beacon Press, 1988), 88–94 (henceforth *TCA* 2).

16. Ibid., 113–18. In addition to borrowing from Max Weber, Habermas also critically borrows from Emile Durkheim's analyses of the social division of labor.

17. Ibid., 137.

18. Ibid., 139.

19. Ibid., 49.

20. Ibid., 189; see also 49–62, 77, 158–59.

21. Ibid., 46–53, 77–94.

22. Ibid., 107.

23. Ibid., 191–96. Numerous Christian theologians, myself included, have disputed Habermas on this point and have offered counterarguments. He apparently has accepted that contemporary Christian theological reflection on the sacred takes communicative reason and action as its own perspective (ibid., 195). For different theological approaches to this issue and Habermas's response, see D. Browning and F. Fiorenza, eds., *Habermas, Modernity, and Public Theology* (New York: Crossroad, 1992). Also see Edmund Arens's very fine proposal in *Christopraxis: A Theology of Action,* trans. J. Hoffmeyer (Minneapolis: Fortress Press, 1995).

24. *TCA* 2 92.

25. Ibid., 145.

26. Jürgen Habermas, *Autonomy and Solidarity: Interviews with Jürgen Habermas,* ed. P. Dews (London: Verso, 1992), 247–55 (henceforth *AS*).

27. *TCA* 2 160.

28. Ibid., 153–72. For Habermas's critical use of Talcott Parsons's general media theory, see ibid., 256–74, and *AS* 261–64.

29. *TCA* 2 155.

30. Ibid., 266; see also FRPS 444.

31. *TCA* 2 270–71.

32. Ibid., 172–90.

33. Ibid., 196, 311–96.

34. *BFN* 186–93.

35. Ibid., 175–76.

36. FRPS 444.

37. *BFN* 295–98. Habermas notes that because the liberal or economic theory of democracy has a loose collection of social norms, it degenerates into a theory of elites, who increasingly suffer from a deficiency of legitimation vis-à-vis the majority of citizens. Citizens then slouch into a reactionary mode of crisis avoidance rather than activist planning and regulating. "Both legitimation deficits and steering deficits push politics into a kind of incrementalism that can hardly be distinguished from quietism" (see *BFN* 333). This situation has led Niklas Luhmann, for instance, to develop a systems theory of democracy. Systems theory considers itself realist because it "cuts the last remaining ties with normative models [and] essentially limits itself to the self-referential problems of an autopoietic [self-regulating] political system, and once again takes up the organizational problems of the classical [economic] theory of the state, translating them into steering problems" (*BFN* 333). The economic theory and systems theory have both "pushed the normative weight reduction too far," Habermas claims (333). He argues that "the normative defeatism to which both lines of political sociology [economic theory and systems theory] lead is not simply a result of sobering evidence but of misguided conceptual strategies as well" (330). Principally, systems theory, with its "autopoietic turn," cuts off deliberative procedures for forming public opinion from their moorings in a political public sphere, in civil society, and in the lifeworld (342). Habermas concludes:

> A systems theory that has banned everything normative from its basic concepts remains insensitive to the inhibiting normative constraints imposed on a constitutionally channeled circulation of power. Through its keen observations of how the democratic process is hollowed out under the pressure of functional imperatives, systems theory certainly makes a contribution to the theory of democracy. But it offers no framework for its *own* theory of democracy, because it divides politics and law into different, recursively closed systems and analyzes the political process essentially from the perspective of a self-programming administration. (335)

38. *BFN* 299.

39. Ibid., 298.

40. Ibid., 299.

41. Ibid., 329–87. To my mind, Habermas has not yet given sufficient attention to this circulation of power's relationship with the economic system. One productive form of investigation would be in reference to economic stakeholder theory.

42. Ibid., 359.

43. Ibid., 360. I have inserted the word "political" into the phrase "the public sphere" because Habermas vacillates between "the public sphere" and "the political public sphere."

44. Ibid., 361.

45. Ibid., 365.

46. Ibid., 367.

47. Ibid. Habermas notes with regard to his own description: "One searches the literature in vain for clear definitions of civil society that would go beyond such descriptive characterizations" (ibid.). In chapter 6, I employ the following definition: civil society is that plurality of institutions, associations, movements, and so on that emerges out of the lifeworld for the prevention and promotion of this, that, and the other thing.

48. Habermas takes up this issue as the "self-limitation" of civil society (ibid., 372–73).

49. Habermas initiates his proposal by examining the mediation between facts and norms within law and legal theory, which remains beyond the scope of this study.

6. Civil Society and Congregations as Prophetic Public Companions

1. Max Horkheimer, *Between Philosophy and Social Science: Selected Early Writings*, trans. G. Hunter, M. Kramer, and J. Torpey (Cambridge, Mass.: MIT Press, 1995), 388 (henceforth *BPSS*).

2. Ibid., 288.

3. Ibid., 326.

4. Ibid., 355.

5. Ibid., 97–100.

6. I pursue this inquiry in the second half of this chapter. It remains beyond the scope of this volume to pursue the other worthwhile question regarding prophetic personality, which is a correlate of this study's congregational focus.

7. For the burgeoning literature on civil society, see John Keene, ed., *Civil Society and the State: New European Perspectives* (London: Verso, 1988); Michael Walzer, "The Idea of Civil Society: A Path to Social Reconstruction," *Dissent* 38 (spring 1991): 293–304; Jean Cohen and Andrew Arato, *Civil Society and Political Theory* (Cambridge, Mass.: MIT Press, 1992); Adam Seligman, *The Idea of Civil Society* (New York: Free Press, 1992); Robert Wuthnow, *Christianity and Civil Society: The Contemporary Debate* (Valley Forge, Pa.: Trinity Press International, 1996); Elisabeth Ozdalga and Sune Persson, *Civil Society, Democracy, and the Muslim World* (Istanbul: Swedish Research Institute, 1997); Tracy Kuperus, *State, Civil Society, and Apartheid in South Africa: An Examination of Dutch Reformed Church-State Relations* (New York: St. Martin's Press, 1999); John Ehrenberg, *Civil Society: The Critical History of an Idea* (New York: New York University Press, 1999); and Andrew Arato, *Civil Society, Constitution, and Legitimacy* (Lanham, Md.: Rowman and Littlefield, 2000).

8. See Walzer, "Idea of Civil Society."

9. For one influential analysis of this situation, see Robert Reich, *The Work of Nations: Preparing Ourselves for Twenty-first Century Capitalism* (New York: Knopf, 1991).

10. Christopher Lasch's account of the family, *Haven in a Heartless World* (New York: Basic Books, 1977), remains flawed precisely because he does not account for the

heartlessness of the family "haven" itself, leaving Lasch unable to locate and access the moral resources that families themselves desperately need. See Patrick Keifert, *Welcoming the Stranger: A Public Theology of Worship and Evangelism* (Minneapolis: Fortress Press, 1992), for a trenchant critique of the ideology of intimacy that infects the familially fashioned congregation and for a promising proposal toward the renewal of public congregations.

11. For a more sustained theology of institutions from the Lutheran heritage, see Gary M. Simpson, "Toward a Lutheran 'Delight in the Law of the Lord': Church and State in the Context of Civil Society," in *On Being Christians and Citizens*, ed. Robert Tuttle and John Stumme (Minneapolis: Fortress Press, 2001). Also see Wolfhart Pannenberg's theological analysis of institutions in *Anthropology in Theological Perspective* (Philadelphia: Westminster Press, 1985), 397–416. Robert Bellah and associates correctly portray the difficulty that many Americans have in understanding how much of our everyday lives is lived in and through institutions (see Robert Bellah et al., *The Good Society* [New York: Alfred A. Knopf, 1991], 3–18). Though much is good in this book, the authors do not make civil society a theme. This remains a major flaw in their conceptualization of "the public church," where "God Goes to Washington" carries the weight of their analysis.

12. I can only offer a snapshot of the cephalous metaphor without its highly complex and integrated, nuanced and normed narrative. According to the cephalous tradition most prominent in North America, the body is not bad or evil per se as would be the case in more dualistic, Manichaean versions. Rather, the body is the seat of the passions, which, left to themselves, are out of control, disordered, and un- or misdirected. In the cephalous tradition's normative account, the head does not enslave the body. That is, the head does not master the body in order to exploit the body for the head's own benefit. That would be tyrannical. Such enslavement would violate the moral norms of the cephalous tradition. Rather, the head cares for the body by disciplining, ordering, and finally directing its passions for the body's own good. In this sense, the head is often presented as selfless, though not disembodied. A disembodied head would violate the moral norm of the cephalous tradition and indeed would lead to the death of the head and the body. The cephalous tradition often exists in close proximity to different forms of love patriarchalism, though it need not. I am developing a comprehensive critique of the cephalous tradition in a collaborative publication with New Testament scholar David Fredrickson.

13. The most influential contemporary version is that of Stanley Hauerwas and William H. Willimon, *Resident Aliens: Life in the Christian Colony* (Nashville: Abingdon Press, 1989).

14. Herbert Marcuse's notion of "repressive tolerance" represents the classic discussion of neutrality as a liberal constraint (see *A Critique of Pure Tolerance* [Boston: Beacon Press, 1965], 81–123). See Ronald Thiemann's insightful discussion of neutrality and toleration in *Religion in Public Life: A Dilemma for Democracy* (Washington, D.C.: Georgetown University Press, 1996), 60–64, 72–80, 159–64. His informative discussion of public reason (121–54) would benefit from our investigations of communicative reason and civil society, and his proposal for revised liberalism is worth considering (95–114). Also see Oliver O'Donovan's criticism of liberalism in *The Desire of the Nations: Rediscovering the Roots of Political Theology* (Cambridge: Cambridge University

Press, 1996). I do have significant disagreements, especially with his immersion in the Western communitarian-cephalous tradition, which lies just beneath his text. The tradition provides significant ballast, especially in his proposal's christological grounding. Still, O'Donovan marshals a wealth of information; especially valuable for the communicative imagination is his retrieval of the open-speech legacy of the fourteenth- and fifteenth-century conciliarist movement (268–70). For a fuller exposition of the conciliarist legacy from the perspective of the history of political theory, see Quentin Skinner, *The Foundations of Modern Political Thought,* vol. 2: *The Age of the Reformation* (Cambridge: Cambridge University Press, 1978), 113–23.

15. See Nancy Fraser's fuller diagnosis of this liberal dynamic in "Talking about Needs: Interpretive Contests as Political Conflicts in Welfare-State Societies," *Ethics* 99 (January 1989): 291–313; and in *Unruly Practices* (Minneapolis: University of Minnesota Press, 1989).

16. Seyla Benhabib, "Models of Public Space: Hannah Arendt, the Liberal Tradition, and Jürgen Habermas," in *Habermas and the Public Sphere,* ed. C. Calhoun (Cambridge, Mass.: MIT Press, 1992), 87.

17. Communicative ethics, as Reinhold Niebuhr did, exercises a double focus on human moral resources *and* self-interested limitations (see especially Reinhold Niebuhr's *Moral Man and Immoral Society* [New York: Charles Scribner's Sons, 1932], xxiv). A fuller Christian, theological account of the communicative moral imagination, which is beyond the scope of this study, would closely connect human moral resources to divine providence and would find a home within Christian approaches to natural law. For a prolegomenon along these lines, see my "Toward a Lutheran 'Delight in the Law of the Lord.'" The subtitle of Niebuhr's book mentioned above is *A Study in Ethics and Politics,* which manifests the weakness of his account. He fails to focus explicitly on civil society as well as on the communicative access to that space.

18. See note 15 above.

19. Here I adapt Dennis McCann's poignant phrase from "The Good to Be Pursued in Common," paper presented at "Catholic Social Teaching and the Common Good," University of Notre Dame Center for Ethics and Religious Values in Business, April 14–16, 1986.

20. For an engaging analysis of democracy and comprehensive goods that critically engages the communicative imagination, see Franklin Gamwell, *Democracy on Purpose: Justice and the Reality of God* (Washington, D.C.: Georgetown University Press, 2000).

21. See, for instance, John W. Dienhart, ed., *Business, Institutions, and Ethics* (New York: Oxford University Press, 2000), 227–70.

22. I borrow the phrase "return of the congregation" and important insights from my colleague Patrick Keifert, "The Return of the Congregation: Missional Warrants," *Word & World* 20 (fall 2000): 368–78.

23. For an insightful account of the history of congregational studies during the twentieth century, see James Wind and James Lewis, "Introduction: Introducing a Conversation," in *American Congregations,* vol. 2: *New Perspectives in the Study of Congregations,* ed. J. Wind and J. Lewis (Chicago: University of Chicago Press, 1994), 1–20.

24. Among this growing number are George Hunsberger and Craig Van Gelder, eds., *The Church between Gospel and Culture: The Emerging Mission in North America* (Grand Rapids: Eerdmans, 1996); Nancy Ammerman et al., *Congregations and Com-*

munity (New Brunswick, N.J.: Rutgers University Press, 1997); Darrell Guder, ed., *The Missional Church: A Vision for the Sending of the Church in North America* (Grand Rapids: Eerdmans, 1998); and Patrick Keifert and Patricia Taylor Ellison, *Testing the Spirit: Congregational Studies as Interdisciplinary Theology* (Grand Rapids: Eerdmans, forthcoming). Core theological practices and critical reflection on those practices constitute the thick milieu within which prophetic reasoning is embedded. I cannot in this study examine those constitutive factors of the Christian congregation. Two others who have contributed to this work from the perspective of critical social theory and Roman Catholic christology and ecclesiology are Edmund Arens, *Christopraxis: A Theology of Action*, trans. J. Hoffmeyer (Minneapolis: Fortress Press, 1995), and Paul Lakeland, *Theology and Critical Theory: The Discourse of the Church* (Nashville: Abingdon Press, 1990). In a forthcoming work with New Testament interpreter David Fredrickson, I employ the communicative imagination to retrieve repressed traditions within christology, ecclesiology, and Christian confessing that constitute Christian missional congregations.

25. I have proposed aspects of this inquiry in three earlier programmatic essays. See Gary M. Simpson, "God, Civil Society, and Congregations as Public Companions," in Keifert and Ellison, *Testing the Spirit;* "Toward a Lutheran 'Delight in the Law of the Lord'"; and "No Trinity, No Mission: The Apostolic Difference of Revisioning the Trinity," *Word & World* 18 (summer 1998): 264–71.

26. H. Richard Niebuhr, *Christ and Culture* (New York: Harper & Row, 1951). I neither rehearse the well-known limitations and problems that accompany typologies of this sort nor offer my own critical reflections on Niebuhr's explication, which includes the nontrinitarian way he frames the inquiry. The benefit of well-known typologies is the clarity they provide and the points of reference they establish in a pluralistic environment. See Avery Dulles's reflections on the limits and usefulness of typologies and models in *Models of the Church*, expanded ed. (New York: Doubleday, 1987), 9–33. Niebuhr himself was aware of these issues (*Christ and Culture*, 43–44).

27. I note one significant caveat as I employ the Christ-and-culture typology. I use the term *culture* in this paragraph in the broad sense that Niebuhr himself used it, that is, incorporating a panorama of human reality, including the great institutions and systems that comprise civilizations. Niebuhr notes that his use of the term parallels how New Testament writers often use "the world" (see especially *Christ and Culture*, 29–32). For an insightful recent consideration of theology and culture, see Kathryn Tanner, *Theories of Culture: A New Agenda for Theology* (Minneapolis: Fortress Press, 1997).

28. Lutheran theological ethicist Robert Benne has employed Niebuhr's notion in *Paradoxical Vision: A Public Theology for the Twenty-first Century* (Minneapolis: Fortress Press, 1995). I differ with Benne's helpful exposition because he thinks of "church" in a twentieth-century manner—that is, too denominationally—and does not account for civil society as a pivotal space of public communicative reason and action. I also differ with his ideological choice of targets for shrill rhetoric.

29. Lutherans developed the servant dimensions of church through their critical theology of vocation. Sadly, the theology and practice of vocation among Lutherans too often became individualistic and privatized and thereby uncritical. For an innovative contribution to evangelization, which in Dulles's typology would appear within the "herald" model, see Keifert, *Welcoming the Stranger.* The two Reformation models need

not be isolated, and ought not be isolated, from facets that the Roman Catholic models attempt to exalt. Reformation theology has enduring contributions to make, especially as it addresses traditionally Roman Catholic formulations out of its own confessional claims regarding the church. Reformation contributions have yet to be made, for instance, in communion ecclesiology. For a provocative contribution from a Baptist perspective, see Miroslav Volf, *After Our Likeness: The Church as the Image of the Trinity* (Grand Rapids: Eerdmans, 1998).

30. For a Lutheran contribution to vocation within the context of political author-ity, see my "Toward a Lutheran 'Delight in the Law of the Lord.'" Noteworthy is how the first two generations of Lutherans developed prophetic reasoning by means of their resistance theory. For the best brief summation of the Reformation doctrine of voca-tion, see Marc Kolden, "Creation and Redemption; Ministry and Vocation," *Currents in Theology and Mission* 14 (February 1987): 31–37.

31. Behind my proposal for a communicative civil society breathes a doctrine of God and creation, of humans in the image of God, and of the Reformation under-standing of sin, evil, and the first use of the law. For preliminary reflections on these issues, see Simpson, "God, Civil Society, and Congregations as Public Companions," and idem, "Toward a Lutheran 'Delight in the Law of the Lord.'" For a handbook on moral deliberation appropriate for public congregational life, see P. Keifert, P. Taylor Ellison, and R. Duty, eds., *Growing Healthier Congregations or How to Talk Together When Nobody's Listening* (St. Paul, Minn.: Church Innovations, 1999). For a helpful analysis of congregations as communities of moral deliberation in the Evangelical Lutheran Church in America, see Per Anderson, "Deliberation, Holism, and Responsi-bility: Moral Life in the ELCA," address at the annual meeting of the Society of Chris-tian Ethics, Chicago, January 2001.

32. See Martin E. Marty, "Public and Private: Congregation as Meeting Place," in Wind and Lewis, *American Congregations,* 2:133–66.

33. For my own exploration of the theology of the cross and the communicative imagination, see Gary M. Simpson, "*Theologia Crucis* and the Forensically Fraught World: Engaging Helmut Peukert and Jürgen Habermas," in *Habermas, Modernity, and Public Theology,* ed. D. Browning and F. Fiorenza (New York: Crossroad, 1992), 173–205.

Glossary

[Note: Asterisks (*) mark words and phrases
that are defined elsewhere in the glossary.]

agonistic: the ethos of civil society that revolves around a "competitive struggle"—from the Greek *agōn*—among rival versions of personal and/or communal moral virtue.

civil society: the vast and pluralistic, interlocking network of spontaneously emerging associations and institutions "located" between the lifeworld* and the two great systems,* forming the organizational substratum of the general public.

colonization of the lifeworld: the potential invasion and destruction of the lifeworld's* communicative rationality by a strategically and instrumentally rational system* previously emancipated or detached from communicative moral discourse.

communicative ethics: an ethical theory based on the insights of communicative reason and action.*

communicative reason and action: the rationality of social interaction that, in contrast to the philosophy of the subject,* takes as its paradigm two participating, communicating partners and the intersubjectively generative power of speech.

critique of ideology: the critical movement to examine and challenge the assumptions, rationality, or ideology* of a given society or dominant societal class, which tend to parade as universal norms.

deliberative democracy: an expression of communicative rationality that, in contrast to both liberalism* and republicanism,* transcends the rationality of the philosophy of the subject.

dialectical theology: the theological conviction, articulated preeminently by Karl Barth, that knowledge of God exists properly only in dialectic, in paradoxes held together by faith, transcending rational comprehension and defying dogmatic formulation.

169

empiricism: an epistemological posture that, in contrast to rationalism,* conceives of the mind as a passive entity, a "blank slate," which simply registers with complete accuracy the senses' experiences of the material data external to the mind.

epistemology: that branch of philosophy that deals with the theory of knowledge and asks such questions as What is knowledge? What are the sources of knowledge? and What are the limits of knowledge?

hermeneutic experience: the participatory process whereby two speakers of the same or different languages (in the latter case, through translation) come to mutual understanding, thus simultaneously demonstrating reason's transcendence of a single language and its inevitable embodiment in the particularities of a language.

hypostatization: the process whereby an abstract idea or attribute becomes concretized into an individual and independent reality.

idealism: the epistemological posture that, in contrast to materialism,* treats ideas and logic from an ahistorical perspective.

ideology: the (often unexamined) system of meanings and ideas within a given society or segment of society and often imposed on an entire society by its dominant segment or social class.

immanent critique: the critical notion that normative rational ideals, which function as standards for critical evaluation as well as for redesigning and rebuilding society, are themselves present (immanent) within the social system, though often in a hidden or implicit manner.

instrumental reason: the conception of reason, contrasting with substantialist/objective rationality,* whereby reason becomes powerful as an instrument or tool for pursuing efficient means toward a given end but impotent for evaluating the desirability or value of the given end or goal.

liberalism: the Lockean conception that the foremost purpose of the democratic state is to safeguard and service a zone called "society," in which citizens exercise their free rights to pursue personal life plans and private expectations of happiness, interacting and struggling with other free individuals in voluntary contractual arrangements.

lifeworld: the constellation of background assumptions of a culture, society, and personality that shape the defining and interpretation of a given situation.

linguistic turn in philosophy: the development in philosophy that, by examining the rationality and practice of language, made possible a greater understanding of noninstrumental space in human life.

linguistification of the sacred: Habermas's phrase describing the transfer of cultural reproduction, social integration, and socialization from sacred foundations to linguistic communication and to action oriented to mutual understanding. Such a transfer constitutes the transformation of the lifeworld* from the realm of sacred, noncriticizable authority to the critical realm of communicative reason and action.*

Marxism: very generally, a philosophical and economic tradition of thought and action critical of the alienation and oppression that are supposed to characterize European, "Christian" capitalism.

materialism: the epistemological theory, contrasting with idealism,* that reason, knowledge, and truth are historically and socially embedded and that any thinking is always the thinking of particular people in particular times and places.

nihilism: broadly, a philosophical trend, characterized by total skepticism, that asserts the meaninglessness of life, tradition, authority, God, or truth.

philosophy of the subject: the outlook, predominant in modern philosophical discourse, that takes as its paradigm a relationship between a subject and an object, wherein the subject has the ability and prerogative to know (that is, to represent to itself) an object and to act upon that object in such a way as to master it.

positivism: any of various philosophical movements that emphasize "positively" certain knowledge gained through rigorous scientific method rather than supposedly dubious knowledge gained either through religious revelation or philosophical speculation.

prophetic criticism: the discipline that critiques the very existence of entire forms and systems on the basis of no fixed criterion, but by that which is beyond all human knowledge, higher than all reason.

rational criticism: the variety of modern, critical disciplines for rationally analyzing cultural, psychological, sociological, and religious structures and conditions.

rationalism: an epistemological posture, typically characterized by Descartes, that, in contrast to empiricism,* conceives of the mind as the only trustworthy source for pure knowledge and objective certainty, untainted by the uncertainty of bodily existence and sensory perception.

reification: colloquially translatable as "thing-ification," a way of life or mode of existence, typical of instrumental reason,* that comes to regard every human reality or relationship as a thing or, in capitalist society, as a commodity, to be known, manipulated, and controlled.

republicanism: the communitarian conception that the foremost purpose of the democratic state is to bring about a political practice in which the positive liberties of equally entitled, participating citizens are realized, such that the state becomes the institutionalization of the virtuous community and seeks an ethical good antecedent to the formation of the state itself.

speech-act theory: also called "language pragmatics," the theory that asserts that language functions not only to represent or affirm reality but that it also embodies and even shapes the social practice of a culture.

substantialist/objective rationality: the conception of reason that, in contrast to instrumental reason,* postulates and seeks to examine an objective, total order within human reality and functions to provide a rationale for the patterns of social existence.

system: with regard to the lifeworld,* the two great structures of the political state and market economy, which are responsible for producing the lifeworld's* required material substratum of food, clothing, housing, and other goods and services.

totalistic critique of reason: the complete and thoroughgoing discrediting of reason as a normative instrument of critique because of reason's supposedly inevitable identity with power and domination.

validity claims: the four claims to legitimacy that all speakers make to their hearers and that hearers require to be affirmed by a speaker, namely (1) *uttering* something understandably; (2) giving the hearer *something* to understand; (3) making *oneself* thereby understandable; and (4) coming to an understanding *with another person.*

Index

Ritschl, Albrecht, 38–39
Roman Catholicism, 6, 43,
    47–49, 62
    and Christ and culture, 142
    models of church, 142–43

Saint-Simon, Henri, 5–6
Scheler, Max, 4
Schelling, Friedrich, 74
Schopenhauer, Arthur, 126
science
    natural, 6–14
    of politics, 12–15
    and scientific positivism. *See*
positivism
    of society, 3, 5–6, 12–15
Searle, John, 78, 88–89
socialism
    religious, 29–31, 40, 50
    utopian, 6
sociology. *See* science, of society
solidarity, 6, 107–8, 114–15, 118,
    121
Soviet Union, 58, 128, 134
speech acts, 88–89
    theory of. *See* theory, speech act
Spinoza, Benedict, 74
state
    absolutist, 15, 17
    and media of power. *See* power,
        administrative
    nation-, 15, 103–4, 135
    system of, 106, 114–22
Stone, Ronald, 28–29
subject, 18, 21, 66
    philosophy of. *See* philosophy,

of subject
    subjectivism, 18–19
    subjectivity, 18, 21, 66
system
    and differentiation. *See* differ-
        entiation
    of economy. *See* economy,
        system of
    of state. *See* state, system of
    theory, 106–7, 112–14, 121

theory
    action. *See* action, theory
    critical, 4, 17–26
    and praxis, 8, 26, 30, 57, 75, 115
    system. *See* system, theory
    traditional, 4, 8–17, 23, 125
    of truth. *See* truth
Tillich, Paul, 27–53, 70, 125,
    129–31
truth, 22
    consensus theory of. *See* argu-
        mentation, theory of
    eschatological concept of, 67,
        97
    fallibilist theory of, 97–98,
        133, 139

utilitarianism, 5–6

validity claim, 86, 90–93
    and practical reason, 98–99

Weber, Max, 55, 60, 64
Wellmer, Albrecht, 86
Wittgenstein, Ludwig, 78–82